The Priest and the King

The Priest and the King

An Eyewitness Account of the Iranian Revolution

DESMOND HARNEY

British Academic Press
LONDON · NEW YORK

Published in 1998 by British Academic Press
an imprint of I.B.Tauris & Co Ltd, Victoria House,
Bloomsbury Square, London WC1B 4DZ

A full CIP record for this book is available from the British
Library

Library of Congress catalog card number: available

ISBN 1 86064 319 1

Set in Monotype Dante by Ewan Smith, London

Printed and bound in Great Britain by WBC Ltd, Bridgend,
Mid Glamorgan

Contents

Acknowledgements   vii

A note on transliteration   ix

Prologue   1

Introduction   4

January–September 1978 The Gathering Revolutionary
  Storm   12

September 1978 The Great Marches and the Jaleh Square
  Massacre   16

October 1978 Khomeini Declaims in Paris; the Shah Dithers
  in Tehran   35

November 1978 Riots and Military Government   53

December 1978 Moharram Marches and the Foreigners'
  Exodus   97

January 1979 'The Shah Has Gone'   136

Epilogue An Islamic Revolution and Its Aftermath   176

Notes   181

Further Reading   202

Index   204

To my wife Judy and daughter Bridget who shared these experiences with me

Acknowledgements

Acknowledgements are usually passed over by the reader but are important to the author as the only means by which he can express his gratitude to those who made the book possible.

My thanks go first to the lady who unwittingly put the thought in my mind of trying to get this journal – by now yellowing at the edges – published by inviting me to give a talk on my life and times in Iran at the School of Oriental and African Studies, London. That sparked the idea.

Then, most emphatically, I thank my publisher, Iradj Bagherzade, who was the first to see there was a book buried in my original text. That was crucial. Iradj has been much more than a perceptive publisher. He has also been an editor with a vision of what the book might be, both as a vivid impression of breaking events and as a work of reference concerning those momentous days. His editorial knife was applied sharply and salutarily to the fat but always stopped short of the lean and never once touched the bone. His particular sensitivity came from having shared in the events himself and from his ability at times to hear himself speaking, as it were, through these pages.

I should also acknowledge my debt to a not entirely dissimilar book on the Russian Revolution which I read many, many years ago but which remained imprinted on my mind because of its vividness and its ability to bring a great episode of history to life. This was N.N. Sukhanov's *The Russian Revolution 1917 – A Personal Record*. I never wrote the diary with the idea of publication but the distant memory of Sukhanov's work was, I suppose, half-consciously at the back of my mind as I found myself too among great events – though as an outsider observing not, like him, as a player.

I am also grateful to those few who read the text and made comments. In particular I invited a sharp critic with an encyclo-paedic knowledge of Iran, and a generalist who knew no more about Iran than a typical newspaper reader, to be frank about it from their respective viewpoints. I felt if it passed muster with them, it would pass muster generally.

I also wish to thank the staff of the library of the Royal Institute of International Affairs at Chatham House whose comprehensive collection of press cuttings of the time proved indispensable.

I end these tributes by paying the highest to Juliet Dryden, then in Cambridge, who endlessly typed and revised my original text on disk with great commitment, patience and skill.

A note on transliteration

There are many systems for the transliteration of Persian, some academically precise but unreadable, others more freehand. I have inclined to the latter for a book of this nature and claim no consistency with any one system. My rule has been to render a word as, in my experience, it is pronounced, for example, *Ebrahim* and not *Ibrahim*.

My exceptions are where, in English, a particular spelling has acquired a right of its own by usage: *Islam* rather than *Eslam*, *Imam* rather than *Emam*. In short, this is a pragmatic rather than a scholarly system, and I crave pardon from the purists.

Prologue

At the time, the Iranian Revolution felt and looked like a true revolution. Now, almost twenty years later, it is clear that this is what it was – a convulsion that overturned an existing order violently, comprehensively and permanently. Nothing else is comparable save its great precursors in France, Russia and China. No matter how it may moderate now, things can never be – Iran can never be – the same again.

Nor do we know whether the wider impact of these changes, of that resurgence of a militant Islam, has yet run its course: whether a century from now these events will be seen as a turning of the tide of history, or merely a threatening wave that never quite broke. We cannot yet know, but certainly what happened in the course of only twelve months from January 1978 to February 1979 was the trigger for events that still reverberate around the world.

Perhaps latent before, simmering just below the surface in many places in the Muslim world, it was the force and fury, the language and imagery, the overwhelming triumph of a mass popular movement, generated and then unleashed by the Ayatollah Khomeini, that began it all. His beard and frowning brow brandished on banners from the Lebanon to Palestine, from the Sudan to Algeria – even to Bradford – regularly still confront us on our television screens. Indeed from nowhere in the course of only a few years, his face has become one of those that characterise our times as seen in such tomes as *World Leaders of the Twentieth Century*.

The Iranian Revolution may in time peter out and come to

seem just an episode, if a prolonged one; but equally we may have seen nothing yet.

It all began in Iran in 1978. The previous order, the monarchical regime that the revolution overturned, had for many years succeeded in deceiving the world into thinking that, unlike so many of its neighbours in the Middle East, it was invulnerable. It had an apparently strong, clear-minded and charismatic ruler who seemed to know exactly what he wanted; it had powerful armed forces, well trained and spectacularly well equipped; it had a massive and reliable income from its oil and gas; and, perhaps above all, it had powerful and substantial support from the West. Even as late as New Year's Eve 1978, President Carter of the United States, less than a year in office as the scourge of authoritarian regimes such as the Shah's, felt disposed to raise his glass to the monarch in Niavaran Palace and say, 'Iran, because of the great leadership of the Shah, is an island of stability in a turbulent corner of the world ... This is a great tribute to you, Your Majesty, and to your leadership and to the respect and admiration and love which your people give to you.'

What then brought the monarchy down? The world was astonished not so much that it did collapse but that it happened with such speed and totality. This book is not the place to discuss the many theories of how and why: that has been done elsewhere. Rather it is an account of how it looked and felt on the ground to an observer who knew something of the country. It is not a strictly day-to-day account but a record of how the most significant events happened and how the muse or mood struck this observer as they did so. I sensed I was living through a great moment of history – and that was the compelling inducement to write it down as it took place.

The book is organised into chapters chronologically. Each chapter is headed by a brief summary of the main events of the month or months it covers; and then those same events are recorded in the pages of the journal. This journal in turn is supported by extensive notes which have the additional effect of serving as a record of when events, often nowadays so imprecisely spoken about, actually took place.

But before we begin, you will want to know something about that person who was the eyewitness.

Introduction

Who, then, kept this diary? Why was he there? What was he doing? Some will know, but for others I should explain that I first went to Iran in August 1958. It did not then enter my head that one day I might be witness to a revolution that would engulf the very society and institutions I was to become virtually a part of. But twenty years later so it proved to be, and this book tells how I personally experienced that revolution as many, many other expatriates did.

The stability of Iran was never in fact as solid as it looked and there had been rocky times before in the early 1960s which, with hindsight, bore the portents of what was to happen later. Even many of the personalities were the same: the same turbulent priest, Ayatollah Ruhollah Khomeini of my title, and the same king, Shah Muhammad Reza Pahlavi.

I first went to Iran in the most junior diplomatic rank of Third Secretary and worked in Chancery, the name in British embassies for the section that deals primarily with political affairs. My task was to analyse and report on political parties and movements, and particularly the communist Tudeh party which was openly backed by the Soviet Union looming across the vast length of Iran's northern frontier. Here I became familiar with the names of many of the personalities who twenty years later were to play such a part in the revolution. I began with some knowledge of written and spoken Persian, having spent a year at the feet of that formidable linguist, grammarian and famous name in Iran Miss Nancy

Lambton, then Professor of Persian at the School of Oriental and African Studies in the University of London.

Iran was still in the later stages of recovery and consolidation after the coup of August 1953 which had restored the Shah to power, but it was poised to embark on that great period of structural and economic development, based on its new-found stability, which was to change the face of the country. It was during this period that the Shah regained his confidence to the extent that he felt able to initiate some key reform programmes that had long been close to his heart such as the land reform and the literacy campaign.

Such steps inevitably proved unsettling by stepping on the toes of long-established interests, one of which was the Shi'a church (the Mosque, that is) as one of the largest landowners of all. The opposition to the land reform in particular – and to other Westernising measures too – was led by a fierce and determined mullah, Ruhollah Khomeini, already well known to his clerical colleagues but hardly known to Iran at large, much less to the outside world. His opposition led to his arrest in 1963 and demands for his execution, but the Shah – astutely at the time it seemed – sent him into exile. He ended up in Iraq at Najaf, where he brooded and bided his time for fifteen years until opportunity for revenge arose.

The old Mussadeq coalition, the National Front, also stirred into life again after its repression following the events of 1953; some of the same individuals who were to be prominent in the revolution, such as Karim Sanjabi and Shapour Bakhtiar, were already prominent then.

During this period I rarely had occasion to meet the Shah and then only on strictly formal occasions. The first time I met him was at the presentation of credentials by the new ambassador, Sir Geoffrey Harrison, in November 1958 at the Golestan Palace. Then each year in March at the time of Norouz (the Persian New Year), came the great formal Salaam ceremony when all the ambassadors and their staffs trooped down to the palace arrayed either in full diplomatic uniform and ceremonial swords (such as ourselves and the Danes) or in white tie and tails (such as the Americans). His Imperial Majesty moved systematically from file to file, and the ambassador introduced each of his staff in turn – a bow of the head, step forward, bow from the waist, smile, step back, bow head again … and retreat. A thin-lipped smile was the most one could expect.

My wife Judy and I left Iran in September 1962 after four years (the morning after a great earthquake – though no portent in this!) and did not return again for almost a decade. But even in this period we followed events from afar by keeping in touch with our Iranian friends, usually seeing them in London on their not infrequent visits to Europe.

We were posted back to Iran again in October 1971, first completing a two-month refresher course in Persian in Shiraz. I joined the embassy finally in late December, this time as a First Secretary and again in Chancery, but charged with a wider brief of studying not only Iran but its influence in the region, including the Persian Gulf, Iraq, Pakistan and, not least, the USSR.

Iran had changed dramatically while we had been away. The Shah/People's Revolution was in full swing (much of it Dr Ali Amini's reform programme under another name), and the Shah had taken a firm grip on everything, down to quite astonishing detail. Material progress was evident on all sides and the growth of Tehran was astounding – the old parts were still recognisable but we also discovered vast new districts not even in existence when we had left.

The Shah was at the apogee of his powers and prestige, having first been crowned and then having celebrated – at the cost of much criticism and even derision, both at home and abroad – the politically romanticised occasion of 2,500 years of monarchy in

Iran which had taken place earlier that year. We found ourselves having to learn a new title for him, Aryamehr (the Light of the Aryans – no hint of Islam, you will note). A worldly wise operator, he had played his oil cards boldly and astutely, revelling in the power and opportunity this wealth brought him and his country.

Whereas previously I had only met the Shah on stiffly formal occasions, I now found myself at times, as did other senior colleagues, accompanying the ambassador on official calls for discreet conversations at the palace (it could be at the Marble Palace downtown, or at Niavaran or even Reza Shah's old palace at Sa'dabad) when there was the opportunity to observe the Shah at close quarters and get some idea of the way his mind worked. Given his interests in international affairs and the geopolitics of the region, he was keen to hear my contribution on East–West relations and how they impacted on the politics of Iran; while the ambassador and I of course found his analysis of any situation revealing.

Apart from these occasions the Shah was also so much more accessible if one chose to study the many extensive interviews he now gave to the world's press. These were often neglected by commentators as mere public relations exercises but in fact they gave real insights into the man, his thinking and his policies.

So much for the king; but what of the priests, the mullahs, of whom I had never met one in all my years in Iran, much less an ayatollah? That alone tells something about the gulf in Iran between the Westerners and Westernised Iranians on the one hand and the mass of ordinary mosque-going folk on the other – a division, a lack of comprehension, that lay at the root of so much that was later to come to pass.

But to return to the Shah who, as I have said, was at the peak of his powers and self-assurance. He could summon foreign heads of state or ministers to come to see him in Tehran or at his chalet in St Moritz at the crook of his finger. Heads of US corporations and other companies, international pundits, academics or journalists, all paid court to him and nodded sagely as he dispensed advice. He relished it, coming across to the Western world as a proud, haughty figure who at the same time was approachable and comprehensible in the way a chief executive or managing director was. This familiarity, even intimacy, with so many world political and business leaders over such a long period made his precipitate fall all the more traumatic. He had seemed there for ever, almost invulnerable.

To his own people, however, he rarely showed his approachable side, preferring to be seen as the traditional aloof, majestic monarch, speaking only in formal orations. Possibly he was aware of himself in these two roles and deliberately chose to adopt the one best suited to his audience: amazingly frank and open to some unknown foreign journalist, reserved or silent with his own subjects as he believed they expected of a monarch.

So enthralling was Iran at the time (even though privately one questioned its real stability when all around us the Middle East was foundering in coup and discord – one simply marvelled and crossed fingers) that for personal reasons I decided to leave the Diplomatic Service in mid-career and commit myself to the country and language that by now I knew best, not least on seeing how marketable it had made me! The occasion was an offer from a leading London merchant bank, Morgan Grenfell, to be its representative in Iran (it had done business there before but had never been represented on the ground) and possibly to blaze the trail for a grand Iran-Arab Investment Bank (which in fact never happened) that had caught the imagination of the Shah. I left the embassy in May 1974 and returned to Iran, an instant banker, only five months later in October.

Now came the shock: I found myself in almost another Iran. No longer in touch with the palace (I met the Shah only once again and that accidentally but amiably on the ski slopes at Dizin), and on strictly business terms with the embassy, I found I was just one of the field of foreign bankers – and a highly competitive field that was – and having to get to know Iranian businessmen, bankers, accountants, lawyers, civil servants and economists, none of whom had been in my ken before except on a personal basis. It gave me a different perspective on things, but I found that, due to my previous 'inside track' experience, I also had an insight into people and policies that others were denied. It opened a few doors (but certainly clinched no deal) and did help me as an observer of the wider game, especially since as I was a former British diplomat it was thought inevitable that behind the scenes I wielded immense influence. For all their country's strutting on the world stage, Iranians still managed to harbour a deep conviction that Britain really did control the levers of power, so was it not obvious that a former British official was still an instrument of British policy and therefore to be cultivated?

My initial years from 1974 to 1976 were during the heady boom, almost a Klondike period, when everyone involved in business worldwide was beating a path to Iran's door (with a handful of notable sceptics and doubters, I have to say). Much of my time seemed to be spent in reassuring nervous potential investors that Iran was not like the rest of the Middle East ... but that, yes, it could all go wrong (though never, I will confess, did I predict that it might go wrong in the wholesale way it did and never from such an unlikely quarter).

Some potential investors thought better of it and went away; others came in and – in retrospect now – after so short a time from start-up, had to pay the price. My impression was that few of the bright-eyed adventurers ever made money out of Iran (or, rather, had time to); rather they shelled out money in reconnoitring the market and completing the long obstacle course of actually getting any project under way.

It was in the course of my new career in business that

progressively I came to sense that all was not well beneath the hectic, glittering surface. Development plans – doubled and then redoubled – overheated and overloaded the system to the extent that it began to fail to cope. Inflation took hold: I saw it through its effect on my household staff and my driver – men in the street who had benefited at every point up to then during the previous ten years. Meanwhile, at another level, quick and big money was being blatantly made and spent. Then there was the daily discontent from power cuts, from tales of the ports and roads becoming clogged up. But as steps were taken to try to lower the temperature, to put a brake on profiteering and wage claims and to single out culprits, the pain spread and with it a sense of injustice and futility.

In the midst of all this a great change came in Washington in 1977 when the Nixon/Ford era came to an end and the liberal, human rights protagonist Jimmy Carter came into office. In Iran, 'liberalisation' was soon not only in the air but on the lips of the Shah himself. Voices began tentatively to be raised from the long-silenced ranks of the liberal nationalists. Few then noticed that the traditional religious elements were stirring too, drawing encouragement from the growing economic discontent among the people and from signs of an easing of political and security controls, and fired by their own detestation of creeping Westernisation, which they saw as undermining both their hold on the people and Islam itself. The record shows that even the best-informed foreign commentators on Iran concentrated on the nationalists and the Left and barely mentioned the religious opposition. But for months there had been growing ferment round certain mosques where radical clerics and thinkers were known to preach. Few noticed it (though taxi drivers did), and even fewer saw it as the first sign of a wave that was soon to break over the whole system, drowning the liberals and the Left (who had always been there) as it swept in. Did even the militants themselves, save for one elderly mullah biding his time in certitude in Najaf, nursing his revenge and his hatred for the whole Pahlavi regime and its Western backers – and single-minded in pursuit of his goal?

Sensing these stirrings as a banker going about my business, there was no more I could do than introduce a greater note of caution in my homilies to visiting businessmen while stopping short of becoming a prophet of doom (I did also happen to be the first chairman of a newly formed Irano-British Chamber of Commerce which did somewhat inhibit me from expressing any deepening unease). As 1978 progressed, my concerns grew, and they became anxieties after the riots in Tabriz in March which signalled the beginning of something that I had not witnessed before. Nothing was ever the same after them. The public order situation steadily deteriorated as the months passed and as our annual return to England on summer leave came into sight.

Once in London in July, I found colleagues in my bank worried, questioning, but able to reassure themselves that the Shah, backed by his army, would be able to handle the unrest and get on top of the situation as he always had before. He seemed invincible to them. No doubt he still did to himself.

My doubts kept nagging and were finally triggered by news on the radio of a terrible fire in an Abadan cinema. A few days later came the so-called Jaleh Square massacre in the streets of Tehran when the Shah's troops fired on massive crowds defying a ban on demonstrations. I decided to be done with leave and to get back to Iran immediately.

Such was my sense that a drama was unfolding that even as I flew in I began to jot down notes. That was the beginning of this journal.

The Gathering Revolutionary Storm

The first shots were fired in Qom on Monday, 9 January in the course of an attack on a police station. Officially six people were killed, a figure revised later to twenty, but rumour soon had it at around seventy.

Feelings had been running high among seminary students at an inflammatory article in the principal newspaper *Ettela'at*, which was close to government. On Saturday, 7 January it had slandered and insulted one of the students' heroes, the firebrand Ayatollah Ruhollah Khomeini, arch critic of the Pahlavi regime, who was then in Najaf in Iraq, in his fifteenth year of exile. Writing too with increasing boldness in Tehran from the opposite camp was the liberal Iranian Association for the Defence of Liberty and Human Rights, consisting mainly of lawyers. Also making his voice heard was another senior cleric, far less radical than Khomeini yet still an open critic of the existing order, Ayatollah Kazem Shariatmadari, resident in Qom.

Serious violence erupted unexpectedly in Tabriz on 18 February on the fortieth day of mourning after the deaths in Qom. For the first time the spectacle of organised attacks on the symbols of Western materialism and modernisation was seen by a startled populace – banks, cinemas, liquor stores and government buildings were the special targets. Officially nine people were killed (300 rumoured) and 120 were injured. After a stunned pause, the Shah reacted not by the expected crackdown but by the dismissal of the provincial governor, the police chief and two other senior police officers. Lessons were drawn.

By late March, rioting had spread to Tehran, Isfahan, Babol and Kermanshah. Wishful-thinkers reasoned that the riots were organised by the authorities in order to create a pretext for the long-awaited crackdown. But this never came. On 9 April a bomb went off at the home of one of the human rights campaigners in Tehran; it was a clear warning not to take things too far.

Throughout all this, the Shah persisted in his public commitment to a more open political climate, on which policy he had embarked with increasing vigour after President Carter's visit over the previous New Year when the latter had famously and fulsomely said, 'There is no leader for whom I have a deeper sense of personal gratitude and personal friendship than His Imperial Majesty.' Opposition to his regime was castigated by the Shah as being the work of 'Islamic Marxists', so giving it a Leftist character.

In a relative lull, Mrs Margaret Thatcher, recently elected as Leader of the Opposition in Britain, visited Iran in late April, by chance on the day after the first of what was to be a series of coups in Afghanistan over the years ahead. On 10 May widespread rioting began again in Qom; the riots were so serious that the Shah postponed his departure on a state visit to Hungary and Bulgaria, an unprecedented step. And the voice of Ayatollah Khomeini was for the first time heard calling for what had never been spoken of before: an Islamic government.

On 15 May Tehran University erupted in riots and was stormed by troops. On 29 May the Shah gave a press conference at which he made his first public comments on the unrest, hinting that 'outside forces were at work seeking the age-old aim of splitting Iran into spheres of influence' – in coded language, seeking to split it between the influence of the Reds and the Blacks, that is, the Russians and the British.

Riots and demonstrations spread on an ever-widening scale through June and July. Shiraz and Mashad became involved. Always the pattern was the same: banks, cinemas, liquor shops and government buildings were sacked or put to the torch. The death toll mounted inexorably. On 6 June the first significant concession to the unrest was made when the head of the hated secret police, Savak, was dismissed.

On 6 August, the Shah in a broadcast gave a pledge of free elections by June 1979; but only five days later martial law had to be declared in Isfahan. By the middle of the month, unrest had spread to the Tehran bazaar, and incidents began to be reported from abroad of demonstrations against, even attacks on, Iranian embassies.

Saturday, 20 August turned out to be a climactic date: at 9.45 p.m. the Rex cinema in Abadan was engulfed by fire and 377 people were incinerated; the death toll later rose to 430. On 23 August, from Najaf, Khomeini published an open letter asserting that the Abadan fire was 'a prelude to a gigantic explosion'. The fire effectively destroyed the reformist, modernising prime minister, Jamshid Amuzegar. He was summarily replaced on 27 August by Ja'far Sharif-Emami, the president of the Senate and a former prime minister from 1960–61. The son of a mullah, it was thought he could be the right man to appease the clerics while being trustworthily loyal to the Shah. But so steeped had Sharif-Emami been in the Pahlavi establishment that he carried not a shred of credibility with the clergy. Still, he tried.

Almost immediately two populist measures were announced dear to the hearts of the mullahs: casinos were to be closed and the hated new 'monarchic' calendar was to be abolished and the traditional Islamic solar calendar reinstated. The situation was not calmed, however, and nor was any breathing space won: on 31 August Mashad erupted in serious riots. On Eid-e Fetr at the end of Ramadan, Monday, 4 September, huge marches, now openly anti-Shah and anti-American, took place in Tehran. For the first time troops on the streets heard the cry 'Soldiers, you are our brothers. Why do you kill people?' Red carnations – soon to become a symbol of the rebellion – were boldly stuck in the barrels of their guns. On 7 September a general strike was called by Khomeini from Najaf and an estimated 100,000 people took part in rallies in Tehran. The day before had seen the first attack on a police station in the capital.

Enough was enough, and on Friday, 8 September, under a statute of 1911, martial law was declared and General Gholam-Ali Ovaissi was appointed as Martial Law Commander. So grave was the situation that the Shah cancelled state visits to Romania and East Germany (which, as it was to turn out, would have been his last).

The ban on demonstrations was immediately flouted and a great mass of people assembled in Jaleh Square in downtown Tehran shortly after nine o'clock that Friday morning. By 11 a.m. things were getting out of hand and the troops were ordered to fire into the crowd.

My journal begins the next day.

SEPTEMBER 1978

The Great Marches and the Jaleh Square Massacre

With the Jaleh Square massacre on 8 September, the pace of events accelerated suddenly. The authorities never truly recovered the initiative thereafter, despite interludes of relative calm. Blood was now seen to be unequivocally on their hands.

My wife Judy and I had been somewhat uneasily on leave in England throughout August. I heard the news of the Jaleh Square massacre on the radio on our last weekend. I decided to return straight away. My journal begins as the plane flies in to Tehran.

During the ensuing month it became clear that this was no passing period of unrest, that immense forces were stirring; and that the authorities had little idea of how to handle them. The first ministers resigned or were dismissed, and the first mention of the Ayatollah Khomeini appeared in the government-controlled press when he was confined to virtual house arrest in Iraq by Saddam Hussein under pressure from the Shah. But few remarked on this at the time.

On 16 September there was a severe earthquake in Tabas, in central Iran, which soon assumed almost symbolic significance as the crack of doom.

SATURDAY, 9TH

Flew in at first light over Tehran. First morning of curfew. Traffic moving, but no fires. Deceptive appearance of normality. Airport not crowded. Took taxi. Tanks and soldiers round the Shahyad[1] and armed sentries at each major intersection. Still, looked precautionary rather than active.

Tales creep in of the massacre of eighty-five people yesterday in Jaleh Square. Helicopters hover and spotter planes wheel. But normal enough ... until the curfew falls. Eerie then. Immediate sense of fear. Each house isolated and lonely, and the familiar streets silent as if it were 3 a.m. They seem a world away though just outside. Only the dogs bark as they would in the African wild when one is safely in camp. Some gunshots. What murder is out there, what schemings, what nervous soldiers?

SUNDAY, 10TH

Life looks bustling and normal in the daylight. Sickening feeling in town about the mounting deaths at Jaleh.[2] Talk of firing from helicopters and of Israeli advisers – untrue, I'm sure. Tales of men refusing orders and firing on officers; or shooting themselves rather than having to fire into the crowd. Of undisciplined conscripts and inexperienced officers. Yet it held firm.

MONDAY, 11TH

(Just off-the-cuff notes on my return.)[3] Am deeply worried about the future here. There is an underlying atmosphere of apprehension and anxiety, overlain by a forced cheerfulness that it will 'all blow over as before' or that 'all will be well once the dust has settled'. There is a certain shock at the speed with which things have deteriorated and at the fury behind the opposition.

It may all calm down but personally I fear it is irreversible. Definitely things can never be the same again. The Shah has lost credibility, is patently on the defensive politically though being tough physically (and inevitably excessively with the human material to hand), and the varied forces of opposition are on the warpath and vengeful. Every day more of the 'old' order (six weeks ago seems like six months) are thrown to the wolves, more past words are eaten, more hasty concessions and disavowals are given, more admissions of the past canker within. Yet the 'new' government is still totally the Shah's creation formed, yes, of tainted men by and large. The opposition has forced a change but has *not* come into government.

Everyone is questioning the army's loyalty under the pressure of shooting down its own kind. The ordinary soldier's closeness to the mosque and the people, his lack of discipline and his officers' lack of battle experience (and fairly ordinary social origins too for the most part) are all being questioned.

Confidence has gone flat. Life as Tehran knew it has gone flat. The curfew, in one way reassuring though it is, makes people fearful and uneasy.

It may all be held by force by the Shah (the family are alleged largely to have upped sticks)[4] and his senior officers' resolve but he has committed himself to freeing the whole system within six months out of a martial law situation. Such liberalisation must threaten to run him out of town if really given its head; and to try to put the lid back on risks an explosion and unacceptable bloodshed.

Not surprisingly, there is a strong anti-foreigner, anti-defence feeling venting itself not only on expatriate executives but even on the foreign domestic and industrial labour force.[5] The US embassy expects a great increase in terrorism if the opposition is again driven underground.

So where do we go? Either further Left, with a rapid deterioration of order if there is any weakness in the army; or else even an Establishment army coup which would probably have to demand the Shah's abdication if its intentions were ever to be believed by the people. So much of what the Shah has built up, politically and economically, over the past years has been thrown on the scrapheap by him himself in response to pressure in the last few weeks that it is hard to see his word ever being taken seriously again. Yet the army might want to keep the monarchy. Nevertheless the Shah's charisma remains despite the grievous blows to it; and it is astonishing – from Macmillan to Stalin – how a strong man can dispose of or disavow his former executives (not close colleagues, mark you) and yet come through. But I suspect this will be a different story.

TUESDAY, 12TH

Some prevalent rumours

- That the British are stirring up the mullahs, their friends of old. The BBC Persian-language service, listened to everywhere, is said to be proof of it.[6] The BBC is coming to dominate conversation. It is the only source of the facts available to all. So what do we (the British) do it for, is repeatedly asked. In other words, is our hand (*dast-e Englis-ha*) behind events and why? This is widely believed at all levels. The revival of an old but ineradicable illusion.
- That the Israelis are helping the army in the street fighting.[7] Numbers go up to 20,000 Israeli troops here. Widely believed among the masses. Who is putting these rumours about so expertly?[8]

Slogans at the great march last Thursday as people who witnessed it tell me

- 'Khomeini is our leader, our Imam, our Shah', chanted by tens of thousands, beating their breasts in near hysteria as at Moharram[9] as they filed past the British Embassy gate in Qolhak. One man was shot as he tried to climb the embassy wall.

- 'Death to the Shah', 'The Shah is a son of a dog' etc. were written on many of the banners.
- 'The Empress is a slut'. 'How much for her tonight?' Films of the Queen seemingly clapping obscene avant-garde performances at past Shiraz Festivals[10] are being shown in mosques to multitudes throughout the country. A shock this, as one had assumed she at least was immune, thought to be honest and caring; but her support of some aspects of modern Western culture has clearly undermined her standing. (All efforts to mount the festival this year were frustrated. Stands and sets were burnt or destroyed the night after they were put up.)
- Allegedly a group of whores – improbably for an Islamic march – carried a banner reading 'Friends of your sister'.[11]

It is becoming settled opinion that the Abadan cinema fire[12] was set by the local police to discredit the mullahs. Crowds are tearing doors off buildings and saying 'So could the doors in Abadan have been taken off' (they were locked). Was probably an Iranian mix-up arising from a police chase of saboteurs – but no one will ever believe this. Another example of this insidious, clever promotion of rumours.

WEDNESDAY, 13TH

This thing is going to explode. I can't see a way out. We are on the verge of a most savage revolution. We have military rule brooding from tanks in the streets while there is impassioned debate in the Majles[13] – words, truths, the like of which have not been heard for twenty-five years. In short, not even the lid has been re-screwed on properly.

It cannot last – and could all happen swiftly when it comes. But there will be greater bloodshed before the army cracks. It would be disciplinarian but Islamic and incorrupt. It need not go communist – but there must be the danger that the Left will prove better organised, more ruthless and more immediately prepared. Or there could be military rule – but without a single Pahlavi,[14] I reckon.

The Shah is said to be dejected, depressed and above all indecisive and confused.

One has a sense of sitting it out, waiting for the bang and hoping one comes through the other side.

The debate in the Majles has been a revelation, a real purgative. It is astonishing to know that there were deputies there who could speak the truth and who had the courage. They may yet save the day, if people can suddenly feel they have an outlet, a means of speaking, a means of finding out the truth.

If the Shah can rally himself and strike down many who are notorious for their corruption, he may yet survive. But one is reminded too vividly of Nixon gradually shedding Haldeman and then Ehrlichman until finally there was no one left but himself.[15] Still, the Shah as king has great mystique. One fears to tamper with the fount of authority. Yet he was the architect and guardian of the system and its executives: he knew its nature.

The silent night passes and with the sun the city comes to life again – and one is tempted to think that it is not so bad after all, that we are all getting too alarmed, and that a show of firmness will bring everything sensibly back to normal in a month or so. Perhaps – if the regime itself were not admitting its own corruption and purging itself while claiming to rule in the name of law and order.

I draw real hope from the debate that such people as Pezeshkpour[16] can hold the centre (and their party is legal already) and stop the thing slipping to the Left. I didn't know they were there – everyone had seemed a yes-man before.

In the next few weeks the Shah – if he has the nerve, resolve and wisdom left in the wake of the personal humiliations due to his *folie de grandeur* – has to see off most of his parasitical family, bring the real culprits of the past to heel, and dispose of Sharif-Emami, himself a pillar of the past order.[17] Then bring in a man who is a true bridge between himself and the real elements of the country, of which a moderate Islam is the most important. Could Amini[18] be such a man, except that he is alleged to be an American tool (he is not) and the Shah detests him? But anyone who is not seen as one of the past pillars.

Then it could be defused, for I do not believe it is the Russians who are out to destabilise Iran – the risks of global confrontation are too great. Unless, of course, they are ready for the big push now, following their probing in Afghanistan, Ethiopia etc? I doubt it – too risky, though without doubt they have the means to try. They will just take advantage of the West's loss.[19] But if the Shah is not sensible, then we are going to have a bloody shambles that could bring the whole Persian Gulf down with it.

Cross fingers.

There is a new saying in town: with the Shah's father, his advisers feared to tell him a lie; with his son, they fear to tell him the truth.

THURSDAY, 14TH

What a miracle this freedom is for the Majles to speak – and for such true men to have been hidden (or cowed) within it. And to allow maximum TV, radio and press coverage of it.

If this is the work of the Shah, he could yet be saved. If it has been forced on him, I have lost all sympathy. It is a revolution in itself. The truth of twenty-five years is coming out – and the people (all of us) are fascinated. The Persian democratic tradition has been preserved and is alive and well, *alhamdolellah*. And we are hearing real Persian spoken again, not the pompous, stuffy rubbish of the old order, but free, humorous, satirical, anecdotal, and fierce. New names, new leaders are already emerging from the shadows – though in the background is the harsh voice of the unruly gallery, a warning. I only hope the Shah is watching his TV. This is the public prosecution of the corrupt. And from the tribune they are speaking to, talking to, the prime minister who takes notes – and through him to that shattered man the Shah, kicking himself for having let things ever get this way. Can these moderates stem the anger? If not, God help us.

The TV switches from Parliament to the Military University where the Shah is giving an address.[20] Everyone watches him, wondering what he is thinking. The audience is as of old – heads bowed, all at attention or with hands folded in front. But he is heavy, dejected, strained, above all sad. Perhaps people feel for him personally enough to save him and will excuse his mis-judgements of people, his romantic but delusory mystique of the monarchy, his good intentions but ineffectual actions rather than his hypocrisy.

Helicopters whirr above my house as he returns from the occasion I've been watching to his lonely palace to face more hard decisions and self-recrimination.

FRIDAY, 15TH

It may seem to be contradicting myself but – short of arbitrary actions – I think the worst is over for the moment. Everybody, from mullah to minister to monarch, has had a shock. But instead of driving the sides apart, it has rallied the solid centre who don't want to see the country torn apart.

Heartened by the inspiration of such free speech in the Majles (like a breath of fresh air), I took further heart from a leading businessman who rushed into lunch today bearing a manuscript 'proclamation' from a leading ayatollah saying that the bazaar could open tomorrow and that the mourning period was over.

Even they have seen – or been made to see by their own brethren – that with another week of business standstill, everyone would be ruined. The whole system had come to a dead stop: no cheques paid, no goods moving. It was ruin for their own people.

If the Shah sees this and responds, much can be saved. But make no mistake: power lies elsewhere than only two weeks ago. He has been brought to heel, his unchallenged writ no longer runs. Yet I sense that such is the feeling of respect for him – a tragic figure for all his mis-estimations and delusions – if he reacts in a conciliatory way now, he could yet save the throne and stability. He is no corrupt bully and people know it. But he is no longer his own man.

One businessman told me that in a town where his factory dominates the scene, he was unaware until a month ago even of the name of the senior local mullah. Yet as early as July he found his workforce, almost to a man, was not under his control but under the control of one Ayatollah Sadoughi. In what way? Because his men were refusing to sign receipts for their wages if they bore the new imperial date. They were insisting on the traditional Islamic calendar[21] which the Shah had set aside only a few months previously. The industrialist huffed and puffed but to no effect. His workers were united. Apprehensive of reactions from the authorities, he had to give way. 'Only then', he said, 'did I realise there was something happening that I had never known before.'

Properly handled this need not be unhealthy. The previous system was corrupt and cynical. It destroyed itself by its own arrogance and insensitivity – and the person of the Shah can least of all be excluded from this. It grew up under him. Patently he is no longer the outright boss: he must listen and heed. The pent-up hatred against the past that is now becoming apparent is terrifying. Here the free expression of the Majles may yet prove his saviour. It could restore faith in institutions and give people hope that they have a voice and a means of redressing wrongs. If he ignores this and tries the strong arm, it will all be over.

So much is in the mind's eye. In the deadened, fearful stillness of the curfew, one is inclined to reach out for any sign that one can perhaps return to the good old 'normal' ways of the past. In my present mood of hope, the soldier 200 yards from my front door, with his automatic and bayonet pointing straight at me as I drive past, and the tank at the road end with the crew crouched behind their machine guns with ammunition belts hanging down, already seem anachronisms.

Iran is not a desert kingdom rich on sudden oil: it is a nation with a long political tradition and, in so many ways, a mature if unruly people. It has been insulted and abused by its own and, given half a chance, will reassert itself. It is good to see the resilience of the centre and of old traditions, whether they be Islamic or liberal constitutional. The danger is that forces have been unleashed, vengeance provoked, which will not accept any compromise.

Later: my still-irrepressible grasping for any sign of hope may prove to be naïve yet again. Talking to my gardener, I first sensed that the wound to the ordinary people, the stunned shock, the hatred arising out of the killings last Friday on Jaleh Square, is not easily going to be overcome. I have never felt anything like this here before. It is the fixed belief in the government's (and therefore, the Shah's) culpability for the Abadan holocaust and the street massacre (now never less than 1,000 dead) on the first day of martial law that is frightening. This has created a gulf between ruler and ruled, even though ordinary Iranians are used to being kicked around and given stick.

There was a look of great sadness and incipient guilt, yet mixed with something of the old contempt, on the Shah's face on TV last night – I can't forget it. It was not the stern look of a man who has righteously had to do his disagreeable but necessary duty.

Can he be forgiven by the majority? There is now certainly a large number who never will. A nasty feeling about.

Later: one is witnessing the rebirth of Iran – through the Majles. The whole population, from grand houses to coffee shops, is glued to the television and radio watching real people, real words instead of the humbug and claptrap they have been used to. It is a revolution in itself. H.I.M.[22] didn't have the confidence to do it before; he didn't allow for love and didn't ask for it. He was too intense, too suspicious, above all too insecure – he was a Nixon figure and is suffering the same fate. Pray that he can yet learn and save himself, his people and his past sincere if misguided efforts. If he is not destroyed physically, he may already be destroyed morally: surely he will be broken or hopelessly embittered.

In my dark moments I fear that too much blood has been spilt, too many errors and deceits have been confessed to – and that the end is yet going to be terrible. Yet the daytime brings new hope that the situation can right itself – unless outside forces are determined to exacerbate it. I believe the Russians are being cautious. Tempted as they must be to push and bring the regime down, they must know this risks general Middle Eastern turmoil and the involvement of the Great Powers on their very doorstep. The Middle East could become the Balkans of the seventies.

Thought: the model should be Juan Carlos's Spain after Franco, but it looks perilously like being Somoza's Nicaragua.[23]

SATURDAY, 16TH

The weekend has passed quietly. The bazaar is to open – but doesn't. There is a sullenness in the air. The shock that was to have worn off hasn't. People are coming to feel that fundamental damage has been inflicted and unforgivable things have been done. There is still a dangerous feeling in the air.

However, fires are no longer burning in the south of town as seen from my office window. Only last week one was wondering when the mobs would sweep north: the tanks have stopped that. From hour to hour one's mood vacillates from a feeling that the system is flexible and will readjust, with life continuing pretty normally, to a sense of the hatred and pent-up violence. From reviving cheer to a certain dread.

Oil is beginning to be mentioned, the old cry. My simple gardener, Goudarzi, tells me that in the mosques they are saying the Shah is virtually giving away his oil to his foreign masters (this, after 1973!). He tells me that his friends are not against foreigners, only the Americans who support the government. 'We like the English very much and' – as if, in his simplicity, he thought I would be pleased – 'the Russians too'!

Two more ministers are thrown to the wolves (and I would be scared this time if I were them with that mob outside howling for justice). One is Mansour Rowhani,[24] for ten years until only last year one of the innermost group of ministers. And there are rumours that even Hoveyda[25] himself is under house arrest. Is this satisfying anyone or yet further undermining belief in the whole regime? Only if the Shah follows it with a bold positive gesture – a free Majles and press – can a new understanding be found.

I still believe that if left to itself the system could, in a rough and ready way, find a new balance. But if the Shah seeks to suppress the movement he has allowed to begin it will explode. And if liberalisation gets out of hand, the army will step in in the classic style, with or without him.

SUNDAY, 17TH

With the end of the confidence debate in the Majles and the further relaxation of the curfew (I and many others are all in favour of a permanent 11 p.m. curfew for a civilised life) I think the present phase is over.

Predictably, 'a Marxist plot' has been uncovered by the government. We will now have that endlessly repeated until it becomes
'fact': explanation by suffocation. Not that one should underrate
the Soviet Union's intentions or boldness, nor its capacity to exploit
disruption. But a calculated plot and forward move like Afghanistan? No. The government's claim is fair enough provided it is
only a face-saving device, but God help us if it is yet again a
means of running away from the truth and reverting in a few
weeks' time to the old ways. I doubt if the mullahs (or the Majles,
I hope) will allow that: there has been a fundamental change in
the balance of power. I doubt if the old game can any longer be
played in quite the same way – even though the nature of the
people, regime and opposition is basically the same.

The first act of a new kind of terrorism began yesterday – nine
soldiers were killed in Tabriz by shots from a patrol dressed as
martial law soldiers. 'Soldiers, Brothers' indeed![26]

The place has been shaken to its foundations – but the walls
have held. Some may be tempted to read Saturday's earthquake in
Tabas, which coincided with a total eclipse of the moon, as a
portent.[27] I hope not.

MONDAY, 18TH

Much calmer. All but normal. How quickly one slips back into the
old ways until it all seems like a bad dream and that we simply
got overexcited! I only hope the same complacency does not affect
the authorities so that they return to tokenism again.

The moderate clergy have reasserted themselves and won back
significant ground. Probably no bad thing. And the centre (including the clergy) has been rallied by the fear of anarchy and
invigorated by a taste of free expression. All to the good – provided
it is not now frustrated. But has this strength been outweighed by
the poison unleashed and the encouragement given to the real

subversives? It will prove to be so unless the centre is supported and allowed to find its own voice. It is up to the Shah – and to good advisers. Perhaps Sharif-Emami is being the man of good sense and moderation that one hoped for rather than the mouth-piece and party-liner. Perhaps. Amini has shown himself too obviously, too soon.

One light on the clergy: much of the trouble is said to stem from the lack of one unchallenged Iranian Shi'ite leader since the death of Ayatollah Borujerdi ten years ago. So there is rivalry between the non-violent, moderate traditionalist Shariatmadari and the demagogic, radical Khomeini.[28] Also it is said that Amuzegar at the outset of his premiership exacerbated matters by puritanically cutting off subsidies and favours to the clergy (among others), a system of patronage of which Hoveyda had been the great master. This does not seem entirely convincing – it may have aggravated matters but hardly created them.[29]

TUESDAY, 19TH

The situation is increasingly normal, yet with many signs that it will quickly and suicidally slip back into old ways. The marches, the riots, the speeches, the placards, however, really happened. It was about to burst if it hadn't been checked.

And our emperor really is seen to have only tattered clothes and to be almost isolated. How can he give even an inch more now? One's instinctive optimism is repeatedly punctured by a feeling of nemesis postponed, of retribution ahead. He is living on borrowed time – but has he any idea of how to use it?

There is a nastiness in the air, a malaise. A feeling that this is a phoney peace, no true normality. A growing realisation that the people are hostile, and that the criticisms and self-admissions and ditchings of lieutenants have brought matters too close to the Shah. Even a tense rumour tonight that Hoveyda – urbane, crafty, sardonic, witty, stylish but frivolous Hoveyda – has been done to death and is not merely under house arrest. Echoes of the murder of Amir Kabir[30] in the Bagh-e Fin. Am certain it is false – but it is a sign of the mood that such rumours can gain instant currency.

How long can this be held? Are we indeed in sight of a great crisis for the West, something that could precipitate a situation worse even than Vietnam? Or is this all too fearful and alarmist?

The radio is full of mourning horns and the doleful chants of mullahs for the dead of the Tabas earthquake.

WEDNESDAY, 20TH

Some tales of the Jaleh Square massacre: three boys being seen riding off on a motorbike – the one in the middle of the sandwich being dead (friends removing his body); or the blood transfusion people being threatened if they dared to give blood to a soldier or policeman. This was the 'two-stroke demonstration': hundreds of Japanese two-stroke motorbikes were used by youths to organise the marches and to pass the word round different parts of town.

Or else the procession coming down Avenue Pahlavi, cheered from the sidewalks, shouting 'This is Avenue Khomeini not Pahlavi'. With a shock one realises how the familiar names and landmarks in life are only held in place by one man or a group of men – they have no being of their own.

Yet for all the hollowness within, there is considerable resilience even in this society, though I suspect it is more respect for the barrel of a gun. Most people want order and prosperity and will stay with whoever can best offer it, no matter what slogans may be chanted; but if a government is thought to have failed economically, then it has lost that prop. The real danger is of general economic discontent among all groups – workers, bazaar merchants and modern businessmen. The consequences of rushing too fast after the oil price rise. It makes the masses susceptible to the agitators.

THURSDAY, 21ST

The Tabas earthquake has been a great distraction. It may even
have pulled the Shah out of his obvious dejection and renewed his
will. But it has also led to competition between the government
relief effort, dubbed 'inefficient and corrupt', and the clergy's own
mosque-directed services, held to be most effective.

The troubles seem to have seeped away through the ground –
which of course they haven't. Easy to relax again in the safe feeling
provided by the now – almost – invisible soldiery. Yet it was only
two weeks ago that one was asking oneself who was friend and
who enemy among the ordinary people on the street – mistrusting
people one would not ordinarily have even noticed.

Foreigners now seem to hit one in the eye more: one can see
them (oneself, that is) in the way that a violent, frustrated, envious,
suspicious young Iranian would, his head full of a thousand
prejudices from mosque or tract. Hostile incidents and glances
barely indicated, particularly among the young in the 'villages' of
Tehran,[31] are more noticeable. It is all there only just below the
surface.

How is the Shah taking it? Are his confidence and determination
returning? And with them an immediate swing back to the old
ways – too old to change? Or is he soured, sick of it all, and of the
renewed efforts required to regain lost ground; and the bitterness
at what he must see as a lack of gratitude, plus despair of his own
people? More and more the name of the Crown Prince is being
invoked by him.[32] Abdication in a year or two? But I doubt if the
regime could survive such a shock unless kept there by the army
for continuity and legitimacy. Sounds improbable.

Once you go outside Tehran – particularly to the south of town
– you realise the present calm is eggshell. It is a phoney peace, not
a truce or a ceasefire. Open disrespect for the imperial family and
things Pahlavi is growing. The situation is held, no more.

FRIDAY, 22ND

A return to the racecourse[33] – reasonably attended, if sparse. Drove back along avenues Farahabad and Jaleh. One had to look to find the burnt banks, but the big new Kourosh store is bombed out as in the Blitz.[34]

Confidence is returning. Begins to look more like an unruly mob that had to be taught a lesson; the rest, gullible people led by the mosque and Left-wing agitators.

SATURDAY, 23RD

The stalemate continues (though as I put pen to paper there is an outbreak of gunfire up near the Hilton).[35] Where is the way ahead? In many ways there already is a military government – and the military will get used to power. They preserve order, and by so doing preserve the system. And Sharif-Emami seems to be playing his political hand quite astutely and firmly. I think we have under-estimated him as a weary old protocol has-been. He is sounding patriotic, the reluctant defender of order (his order, of course) and good sense. He may prove a conciliator – and hence a first target for assassination.

MONDAY, 25TH

There is much talk of growing industrial unrest. Workers and staff are taking advantage of the situation to demand higher wages and benefits. *We kept quiet up to now* (as they largely had done) *and we want our reward.* This is not politically motivated unrest, but springing out of widespread economic discontent. The authorities are already conceding across the board – so ensuring an early increase in inflation again.

But the bazaar is back to work and money is circulating – largely by fiat of Ayatollah Shariatmadari, not the authorities. The continuing crucial importance of the bazaar and its closeness to the mosque has clearly impressed the government.

Many feel that only action on corruption has calmed the situation – but that the advantage will soon be lost if no further action follows. Just the same charade? If not, where does it stop?

The organisation of last Friday's riots seems to have been largely in the hands of students rather than locals or mullahs. The rioters threatened to overrun the town if they had not been shot down. Generally agreed it was truly touch-and-go for the regime itself that day.

The BBC Persian Service has become a big factor. There is a rooted belief that the British are fomenting the trouble, and the BBC – widely listened to and believed – is the evidence for it. In fact it gives a fairly straight reportage, if sympathetically inclined in tone if not in fact to the liberal opposition. Its power is that it is in Persian (and therefore widely accessible) and is the sole source of full and fairly objective reporting.

The period ahead that people are already talking of with dread is the beginning of Moharram (mid-December). After that, there will be only a few months to the 'elections', with every joint in the body politic then strained or dislocated. But one must hope that if the great powers continue to stand back (above all that means the Soviet Union) – as I believe they will – the Iranian Establishment can sort things out for themselves, if in a very rough way; and that they will only dispense with the Shah if they have no alternative. The worst outcome is that the accumulated problems and self-deceptions are just too large to be soluble by orderly means. At such times I continue to hope.

WEDNESDAY, 27TH

A foreign banker colleague who has lived and worked through most of the Beirut civil war said that curiously he finds the build-up to martial law here more alarming than anything in Lebanon. There it had been community against community in specific areas of town with no anti-foreign feeling as such – people only got harmed if they were caught in the cross-fire. But here he feels a general xenophobia, a real fury and anarchy just below the surface. Unsettling!

A sober, responsible, loyalist Iranian who witnessed the famous Thursday (7 September) march said his confidence in the future of the existing order had been shattered by that one sight of such mass passion and discontent: he couldn't see how it could be appeased or permanently held down by the military – who would themselves crack if called upon to do again what they had to do at Jaleh Square.

Everyone feels great changes ahead.

OCTOBER 1978

Khomeini Declaims in Paris;
the Shah Dithers in Tehran

October was a month of steady deterioration as the Shah and the authorities progressively lost control and were unsure how to react; the revolutionary forces engaged in a mounting campaign of civil disorder, and brought off what turned out to be a crucial move by bringing Khomeini to Paris from Iraq.

The Shah sought to have Saddam Hussein restrict the activities of this troublesome priest but not to expel him. However, Khomeini himself suddenly decided to quit Iraq and was persuaded to come to Paris. On his arrival on 6 October the Ayatollah, now more accessible than in dusty, sleepy Najaf, quickly started to exploit the world media to his advantage and the whole crisis escalated.

Sharif-Emami remained prime minister but beneath him more and more of the Shah's men were dismissed or resigned. Meanwhile the most potent weapon in the hands of the revolutionaries proved to be the strike. The first general strike called by Khomeini from Paris on 16 October was widely observed.

Riots spread to many towns throughout the country and the death toll mounted. The pattern was always the same: attacks on banks, cinemas, liquor shops – the symbols of the Western materialism that had spread in the country in the boom years, actively encouraged by the Shah. Openly the cries were now 'Death to the Shah' (Marg bar Shah) and 'Greetings to Khomeini' (Doroud be Khomeini).

SUNDAY, 8TH

Signs this country is becoming nigh ungovernable. Strikes –
unheard of six months ago – are plaguing all sectors and the
government is swiftly conceding wage demands of 25 per cent,
even 50 per cent. We are in for roaring inflation again although
the Shah claims that compensatory cuts in expenditure have to
come out of the defence and nuclear programmes (he is making
them the scapegoats when in fact they were to have been cut in
any event for political as much as economic reasons). University
students are refusing to attend classes. And a new minister has
resigned when he saw that the scope of the reforms required was
quite beyond his administrative machine.

Elsewhere violence repeatedly erupts in parts of the town not
already under martial law. Selective arrests of liberals continue, as
well as the bringing to book of 'fat cats' and former power barons
– some very close to the Shah. Each day the shadows seem to
creep nearer to Hoveyda himself.

It all looks pretty insoluble and the classic prelude to a revolution. I believe the problems are insoluble by the present men and
that the popular forces that have been unleashed – both the
opposition elements that at long last have seen their chance as
well as the subversive elements that are taking advantage of it all
– have the initiative and will keep up the momentum until some
conclusion is reached. And that will still probably be a military
government despite the liberal noise and fury. But of what kind?

MONDAY, 9TH

Among the people at all levels – from taxi drivers to high society
– the unsayable is being said more and more: the Shah must go.
People are becoming bolder in saying this, yet are fearful of the
consequences. The conviction is growing that the web of false
assurances and promises will not be broken until he has gone;

nothing under him any longer has credibility. A terrible thing to say when he has done so much: but the truth. Some even question whether he has the resolve to stay or whether he might not flee as he did in 1953,[1] washing his hands of the mess his people have made. I don't believe it: he's a sticker this time. Unrealistic and arrogant he may be, but he is sincere and a patriot.

People are beginning to reveal their true colours. There are even the first detectable signs of reinsurance – but with whom? For there is the rub: there is no single opposition. And what opposition there is is united in only one thing: their opposition to the present regime, not in agreement on any alternative pro-gramme. The age-old problem. People talk increasingly of the necessity of a military government. But again, what military, which officer? The present High Command are not exempt from the charge of being corrupt place-seekers simply because they are in uniform. The fall of almighty General Nassiri of Savak is seen by many not as an isolated case, mightiest of all though he was.[2] Indeed the nationalists are looking to the colonels and brigadiers as their potential friends, and keep showering the martial law troops with flowers – until they shoot. The people know who alone bars the path, and imagines it (the army) to be vulnerable; but there are no sure signs as yet that it is.

Already the radicals – above all Ayatollah Khomeini, now trans-ferred from Najaf[3] to Paris – are setting the pace, and the local mullahs are panting to keep up. The return of Khomeini could be a traumatic event and would lead to popular pandemonium. I doubt if the Shah could survive it; he would rather leave. That would be one of the two events that would make him go if he was pushed that far; the other would be if he was asked to leave by the military for his own good and the good of the country.

The thing is on the move – one can feel it – and the authorities are either paralysed or surrendering. Hence the wave of industrial unrest and wage demands.

TUESDAY, 10TH

One senses the day drawing in – an 'end is nigh' feeling. I give it another month in the sense that the Shah has that time at the most in which to set a new course: either he stands back and gives someone new (Amini? General Djam?[4]) the effective helm; or else he tries to crush it and put in another Establishment man or the provocative, unacceptably hard-line Zahedi.[5]

If the latter, it will blow up in his face and the end could be terrible. If the former, there is some hope. If no one will even attempt to allow the Iranians the chance of constitutional democratic government, then one can never know if they are capable of it or would only pull themselves apart. It is the only way they can mature – risky period though it would be. Karamanlis did it in Greece; Suarez is doing it in almost equally difficult circumstances in Spain. I suppose Portugal is more of a parallel. But none of these had to contend with the fury of Islam, nor with the irresponsibility and selfishness so endemic in Iran.

Day by day the situation is deteriorating, especially now that the disillusioned firebrand students are back in the universities. Trouble has moved up from the south of town into the main streets. Pahlavi Avenue was full of chanting students this morning, edgily watched by troops behind gleaming ammunition belts hanging from their burnished machine guns. Car sirens wail and helicopters clatter and roar overhead – habitual sounds of the last few weeks. Why, after all these years, are there no riot police? Armed troops escalate matters immediately, even though they are an undoubted deterrent.

WEDNESDAY, 11TH

The degree of outspokenness against the Shah is astonishing. Suddenly, at every level. The throne itself is seemingly under negotiation. It is said the demand from the clergy working through Amini is that he should leave for six months while the Empress and son hold the throne (he would never come back, of course). He, equally predictably, has refused; but he must be so lonely, so isolated, so confused, so bitter.

A witch-hunt is on. Unknown people are visiting government agencies and soliciting criticisms of their superiors from junior staff. If this does not satisfy them, staff are telephoned anonymously asking them to report dirt on their superiors. Heads of agencies, respected men loyal to the regime, find themselves smeared and threatened with dismissal or, worse, disgrace and even arrest by agents of their own government. We are witnessing a revolution in slow motion – inexorable, unjust, if at times just. There are many, however, who would like to speed the film up.

Another analogy is of the tide coming in. Hasty bulwarks have been thrown up but the water finds its way through and around. New men with different ideas are appearing in the places left empty. Oh, for a clean, clear change of government – but regimes are more than governments.

THURSDAY, 12TH

How one's memory goes back over the years when so many people, especially the ordinary people, would say (until it became entirely predictable) 'Our quarrel is with the people round the Shah, his family, his advisers, not the Shah himself.' And one knew – but refrained from saying – that they were either deluding themselves or were deliberately muffling the point out of prudence. Anyone at all close to the Court knew that all decisions, approvals and appointments stemmed from him. It was (is) his Court, his monarchy, and the whole farrago of the 2,500 years play-acting and the annual celebration of his 'miraculous' escape from the foul traitors' bullets was his doing; and that if his sisters and brothers got up to as much as they patently did, he was either remiss in not knowing or else too indulgent. And everyone knew that he kept himself better informed than almost anyone – with the big caveat: that he believed only what he wanted to believe and was told only what it was thought he wanted to be told.

So he seems at an impasse. Every day that passes, more of the initiative passes to the wilder men, above all to Khomeini (intimidation squads are visiting leading businessmen in town and demanding that they should stand up and be counted. If they don't and speak ill of Khomeini or well of the King, they are told to wash their mouths out). If the Shah is to save not merely the situation but himself, he must make a bold move, over the heads of the few 'safe men' left to him, to men who have truly widespread support. Only then can the monarchy be saved. But can he bring himself to? I fear he can't. It requires too much of a change of attitude, too great a swallowing of pride.

This to some extent must be coupled with a direct appeal to the people on TV and on the radio. He must still be seen as the assurance of stability and legitimacy, if less as a man than as a symbol (though his face and bearing have become part of Iran). Many might then respond. But this too is what he has always failed to do. He has eschewed demagoguery, right; but he has also denied himself the help of love, of a people's personal identification with a leader. He has been deliberately aloof, remote, humourless, stiff (despite the happy family snapshots). That is his domestic image, quite unlike the more personal, approachable national managing director one sees on TV screens in the West.

So if you ask me what my bones tell me, it is that he is going to find it very difficult to change; and that therefore the prognosis is not good. And God help us with what follows in those circumstances – quite different from what *might* follow if he allows the liberal nationalist centre to show itself (unpleasant though this would also be in many respects, but the old palmy days for the West are over in any event). The next month, before 2 December at any rate (the beginning of Moharram), looks like being crucial.

Strikes on all sides. No newspapers because the authorities tried to crack down on the *Tehran Journal*[6] for publishing a photograph of Khomeini on its front page, and the staff walked out (what a mistake has been made in driving that man out of relatively obscure exile in Iraq to a worldwide platform in Paris). The Hilton went on lightning strike at 4 p.m. representing all leading hotels: 40 per cent on wages and masses of fringe benefits. The usual futile arguments about effects on employment and inflation were being deployed against the strikers one day – then all demands were conceded twenty-four hours later!

SUNDAY, 15TH

Best to get our minds clear on what forces really are at work, what is cause and what effect, because we are in the myth formation period. According to the authorities everyone seems to be destabilising the place – the Russians, and also the British (especially the BBC) and the Americans and the oil companies, all for different reasons. They have half come to admit the main fault may lie in themselves, but Iranians are always tempted to shelter behind the explanation of outside forces.

Elements in the authorities are beginning to call for 'a line to be drawn', pronouncing 'enough's enough' etcetera, particularly in relation to wage claims and the freedom of the press. Concessions should not be made under duress, etcetera. Ideally, correct. But if 'concessions' are made at the right time, one never should get into a position of duress! And, whatever they say, the Shah has been making concessions under duress since July. Of course this is leading to demands for more and encouraging the Left. Yet what alternatives do they have? Sadly they are on the run. Only today they suffered a signal defeat: they had to surrender in the newspaper strike over press censorship.[7] The authorities have caved in after four days.

What are the Russians thinking of all this? Rubbing their hands and hardly having to do anything, I would guess. I still maintain that outright destabilisation of Iran is too bold for them at the moment – unless they are ready to take on the West in a confrontation over a crucial area. But to have the Iranians of their own accord weakening a key position of the West can do nothing but give them satisfaction.

MONDAY, 16TH

General strike of shops, almost totally observed to commemorate the fortieth day[8] after the Jaleh Square massacre. A great show of military force ensured that there was no serious trouble (though there were some deaths reported in the provinces). A day that began with one grasping for hope that it was all calming down again and that sturdy old Sharif-Emami would see us through, and in the evening anxiety again that the whole thing is on the brink of violence.

One school of thought encouraged by Ardashir Zahedi – who is obviously very close to the army leadership – is that the 'fever' will soon pass, and that if it doesn't then sharp, firm action will settle matters. This school seems to have little time for Sharif-Emami who is seen as a typical politician giving in to popular and Left-wing pressures. They are said to be incensed at his 'surrender' to the journalists in granting press 'freedom' which led to the humiliating ousting of the martial law censors (army officers) from the *Tehran Journal* offices.

One even senses that in many respects the army is already in the driving seat and that the Shah is torn between heeding their wishes and trying to keep alive some embers of his 'liberalisation' policy. Meanwhile Carter cheers him on, not seeming to realise the real forces at work.

Journalists are flocking into town and taking up much of the valuable time of the likes of Zahedi, Shariatmadari and others. Apparently Liz Thurgood[9] of the *Guardian* was expelled because she filed the story (widely believed to be true) that relatives had to pay the army doctors 500 tomans for every bullet extracted from the dead after Jaleh Square (they have to be removed before a pure Muslim burial can take place).

Amini seems to be making a bit of an ass of himself. He is too eager and really doesn't carry confidence with any one of the contesting interests. But, at seventy-three, he's a wise and wily old bird. Sharif-Emami grows in stature. A solid but sturdy Turk. Essentially I believe him a moderate and a Muslim conservative. It is just that he has to earn the people's trust after so long being a pillar of the Establishment. He has won the press over with his leadership on censorship, however. I fear he will ultimately satisfy neither Right nor Left, but he seems the right choice for this phase.

I increasingly suspect that we are approaching outright military government. The press will no doubt soon abuse its freedom, or the Majles will get out of hand, or there will be terrorist incidents – and the army will then surely step in overnight. They will keep the Shah if they possibly can (although I doubt if even now he is in league with them like a Somoza – they say he is personally deeply affected at the killings, even of rabble-rousers); but if not, he will be removed and at best the dynasty will be retained for legality and continuity. One can imagine personal ambition already stirring in one or two breasts. But whose?

THURSDAY, 19TH

The fortieth day of mourning (of Jaleh) was surmounted with little trouble in Tehran and only scattered riots in the provinces (sixteen dead) due to a classic show of force. The situation has now become political again. Sharif-Emami, the man who holds the bridge, is being kept at a distance by some who believe they might be smeared by association with him and who think they have a chance of their own. Thus opportunistic Nahavandi,[10] still trying, quits on a part-conservative, part-liberal issue. He must still be a favourite of the Shah's (at any rate) as a 'liberal' alternative. Then there is Zahedi, at heart the army's man, but bidding for the liberal and the clerical vote too. His time has not yet come but he has well and truly hoisted his flag.

FRIDAY, 20TH

I find no one who supports Zahedi. 'Unacceptable' is the word generally applied and no one can take Nahavandi seriously – he also is seen as too much a creature of the Shah's. For there is the rub: the finger is pointing too much at H.I.M. himself for sheer bad management and 'bigheadedness'. Many want him out; the moderates (so-called) are prepared to keep the Crown Prince, provided the dynasty allows a genuine political debate to develop. Many fear the army which no doubt could succeed but could achieve nothing constructive. But who would be their front man – Djam? He's a worthy, respected figure from an old family, but with no civil or political experience – a fine scholar soldier.

What is emerging – but still only faintly heard – is the voice of those middle-class professionals and technocrats who are the product of the last twenty-five years. One has always said they wouldn't brook autocratic rule for ever, particularly when it makes a mess of things; and now this is happening in front of one's eyes.

MONDAY, 23RD

From further conversations, I think I have been thinking too wishfully. My generation of friends – now the heads of government agencies, banks, technocrat ministers, academics – show little inclination to put their heads above the political parapet. Wearied of it all, they say the initiative lies with the young. Thus even they pass the buck.

In many ways we already have two societies: the Establishment on the defensive and, ranged against it, the totally disaffected bazaar, the students and the religious. At the universities the students have divided themselves into 'communists' (calling themselves that openly, not Tudeh) and 'Muslims'. There is already animosity between the two – seeds of bitter conflict if the opposition were ever to come to power. One feels the whole order breaking up. Solid middle-class people talk disconcertingly of the Shah and his regime as if it were already a thing of the past. Eerie. The degree of criticism of the Shah at all levels is astonishing. People feel free at last to say what they have obviously been thinking privately for years.

On the other hand more and more is heard of the National Front (Jebhe-ye Melli)[11] which is spoken of as respectable, anti-communist, containing good men, etc. But above all of Khomeini – the radical charismatic Islamic hero. There is no other name to match his in emotional appeal. Strange to think of the destinies of this country being swayed by a frail, elderly, vengeful priest sitting in a Paris suburban villa, with half the Iranian world paying court to him there!

David Owen[12] was incautious and unwise in his statements in support of the Shah. Let him speak strongly in support, yes; but don't deride, disparage and sneer at the 'fanatics' of the opposition. His statement polarises the situation in a distorting way and shows him badly out of touch (advised presumably by the British Embassy under intense pressure from the Shah). The trouble is the latter are leaning too far the other way to compensate for the BBC Persian Service – which is listened to avidly and admired by almost everyone one meets. One finds oneself almost basking in the reflected glory of Andrew Whitley (the local BBC correspondent).

More dreadful killings today – forty dead in Hamadan. What an insane policy. They have spent billions on stupid F14s and F16s that they'll never fly against an enemy; but against the only 'enemy' they are likely to meet, they have only nervous troops and no riot police. Each incident is like sticking a banderilla in an already maddened bull – but this bull could yet kill the matador.

How can it ever be solved in this way?

TUESDAY, 24TH

My first visit to the Majles-e Shaura.[13] A French form of chamber with tribune and semi-circular benches. As might have been expected, constant movement and noise. Like an airport terminal with messengers here, bows and waves to friends there, deputies in and out, crossing the floor, constant raising and lowering of desk tops, even two photographers strolling about to get the best angles.

Yet nevertheless an Assembly, with all the fascination of watching any such group of people and espying the notables. Equally predictably the loudspeaker system was more for amplification than clarification. Speakers usually harangued the microphones with great force and speed, racing through their written texts. But here and there was a more considered speaker and attentive audience. Considered or not, the President (Speaker) would interrupt abruptly and that was the end of that, even in mid-sentence. Once when he spoke into the microphone over an opposition deputy beginning to criticise the Shah, several deputies erupted in anger.

Two touches: a busy little bespectacled and bearded mullah in robes who came up to the Chair and spoke earnestly and forcefully into the Speaker's ear (the photographers saw the symbolism and snapped quickly). Incidentally, a surprising number of women among the deputies. As I left I peered into the gardens at the back of the building only to find soldiers reloading machine guns and counting the rounds in their belts. And as I emerged onto Parliament Square, I found myself facing armoured cars with their guns at the ready covering every corner of the square.

These are excitable, critical times with everything on a knife edge. People don't know whether to laugh or cry – but what smile remains is slowly being wiped off their faces. What a miasma! How hopeless it all seems. All the more so the closer one gets to the top. There seems a paralysis of thought and action. Just a holding operation – which day by day seems to hold less and less. Each day a new town erupts into violence as belief in the determination of authority weakens.

This is the recipe for revolution that one has always read about: that there seems no way out – and yet things have to go on. Then at some point the pressure and strain becomes too much, and there is a crack. When? How? By whom? One can only see a general breakdown of order and discipline unless the Shah leads and gives power to some trusted man or group.

The scale of corruption daily becomes more apparent – and clearly it encompasses the senior officers just as much as the others. The officer corps too has long since been weeded of independent men, so that any coup is not going to come from the senior officers. They are terrified of responsibility. But can those called upon to shoot (i.e. the troops) and to order the shooting (the middle-ranking officers) be relied on indefinitely? If not, the mob will go on the rampage and it will be impossible even for the moderates to restrain them. The army itself is Muslim, and lower-middle- or working-class by and large.

I cannot see that the Shah can change his attitudes and habits. His sense of insecurity, his jealousy of talent, his refusal to listen to the truth – even if anyone dared to tell it to him (and those that did ensured their own removal) – are so clear to see. How can a man like that change after thirty-seven years? Yet he cannot master or even placate the forces now at large. Hence the sense of hopelessness.

No one wants a theocratic state, an Islamic government. There never has been such a thing in all Iranian history. But the *ulema* (clergy) have always been the ultimate guardian of the Iranian soul – slow to move, but irresistible when provoked. And the provocative article insulting Khomeini's family and background did it.[14]

WEDNESDAY, 25TH

Hamadan, Gorgan, Qom – the roll call of riot-wracked towns increases. Through the office windows come the shouts of marching students, groups of a hundred or so from local colleges. The people seem maddened (although at any one time most look normal) and want to be rid of the whole charade.

Someone remarked that the generation who had known the violence of Mussadeq's days, and were cautious because of it, are now too old. Twenty-five years had passed and a new generation had taken to the streets – just as with those who knew the Great War and those who did not. Everywhere people talk of Khomeini. And there he is in Paris, no doubt wondering at everything about him for he had never been outside the Muslim world before. The poor French Embassy here – each day flowers and bouquets are delivered to thank them for their hospitality to the Ayatollah! And hapless Giscard[15] is no doubt under the whip from the Shah.

As is our embassy too, continually. For this is the BBC revolution. Every man-jack Iranian is listening to it and we find ourselves popular heroes. Most people believe that this is our real word and dismiss David Owen's statement as a deliberate smokescreen.

Another exciting factor of these days is the press. Overnight as it were, they are their own people and one can sense their new sense of mission. The newspapers are suddenly worth reading – even though there is clearly great self-restraint still being shown. Nothing overtly against the Shah is yet being said.

Jokes of the crisis:

- Half an hour before curfew a man comes running past an officer and a soldier on duty. The soldier raises his rifle, shoots and kills him. 'What have you done that for?' the officer demands. 'Oh, it was only Ahmed Ali, the bastard. He lives so far away, I knew he'd never make it in time.'
- A soldier in the turret of a tank behind his machine gun. The crowd rushes at him. 'No rush, no rush,' he calls out. 'Plenty of bullets for everyone.'
- The Shah boasts: 'When I came to the throne there were only 16 million Iranians, and now there are 35.' 'And the way things are going,' goes the retort, 'there will only be 16 when you leave it.'
- When the Chairman of China, Hua Guo-feng, called on the Shah, the latter asked him how many dissatisfied people he had. 'Oh, 2 to 3 per cent,' replied Hua. 'What would that be in numbers, then?' the Shah enquired. 'About 30 to 35 millions,' said Hua. 'Ah ha, then we each have much the same problem,' retorted the Shah.[16]
- The Rex cinema in Abadan where over four hundred people were burned alive – 'Kebabi-ye Aryamehr' (the Shah's Kebab House) it is being called.

SUNDAY, 29TH

A walk through the campus of Tehran University. Scruffy with revolutionary slogans sprayed or daubed on every available wall. Tree boles covered with pinned proclamations, surrounded by knots of craning readers. By the main gates, a noticeboard bearing colour photographs of victims of street shootings. The whole place politicised and the atmosphere charged. A separate world of revolutionary activity.

Most slogans praised the Islamic movement ('Freedom and

Islamic government'), and friend Khomeini has been elevated to the sanctity of an Imam. His was the name everywhere, with little evidence of direct anti-Shah slogans. The Shah's statue still stands serene (none has been toppled yet that I know of) but the inscription on it is defaced with slogans. Like the regime itself – just short of a direct attack, but getting near it.

Many girls were in full black veils, and many more – most in fact – in the now common headscarf.[17] Many students were in the mosque while others were praying on the lawns outside. No obvious security men inside, but police waggons stood outside the gates and an occasional truckload of troops drove past.

MONDAY, 30TH

'It can't go on like this', 'It can't last in this way' are the comments on everyone's lips; but there is also bafflement and growing apprehension as to the way it may go. Each day of indecision means the country becomes polarised between the security forces and the revolutionaries, with the mass support there is now patently behind them.

I have a growing apprehension of something terrible: the power of Islam as it hasn't been seen for generations. One knows that Islam is resurgent everywhere – Pakistan, Egypt, Indonesia – but here it seems so furious, menacing, determined. Khomeini's intransigence is becoming frightening in its rigidity. I heard one comfortable theory advanced that he and Shariatmadari were hand in glove, with Khomeini agreeing to take a hard line so that the 'moderates' could use his obduracy to extract maximum concessions. I can't believe it is so orchestrated.

Khomeini's single-mindedness on being rid of the regime and the monarchy is daunting. Islam is emerging as an all-powerful force that recks nothing for the supposedly puny communists and is fired by indignation, medieval pride, burning faith, and nationalism. The university campus and its praying youths tell it all. These people, if they sweep through, will burn all and purify the country ruthlessly. But surely it couldn't happen here? Or could it?

How can Khomeini be isolated and the moderates conciliated? For if they are not, we are in for nemesis. I was told tonight that chain telephone calling has begun: a call to require fealty to Islam, with the order to ring six others – so powerful and pervasive is the organisation behind all this. Even the Russians must be worried at such a movement. What effect could a religious explosion have on the Muslim communities in the old Iranian lands (Central Asia, the Caucasus)? It must give even them pause to think.

The chances of the Shah – and with him the whole monied, urban class who still shake their heads in disbelief at what threatens – seem to grow shorter and shorter. It is his paralysis of action, his virtual disappearance. The rats are now nibbling: his portraits are being surreptitiously taken down in shops, whether from prudence or intimidation. His statues are being defaced – but not yet toppled.

It is said the Empress is proving a prop and support, though shocked and frightened at the demonstration of her own unpopularity after all she had done for social welfare and culture. The Crown Prince, eighteen today, is doing a jet fighter training course in the US – somehow symbolic of the distance between the regime and the people.

If it was only the Left I would be less frightened – only worried. But the sense of this tenacity, rigidity and fury of Khomeini is unsettling. Nor is there any doubt where the common people stand ('ignorant', say some, 'don't know what they're doing' etcetera), as common people and mobs – the great catalysts of history – have ever been before.

Meanwhile, the economy falls into paralysis. Strikes are rampant, near-anarchy prevails. The Minister of Finance was locked out of his own office by his staff today. The entire oilfields are on strike. Gangs of students roam the town forcing the closure of schools. And everywhere, killing – ten, twenty or more, each day. Even a Kurdish horseback raid today which left twenty-seven dead. The place seems to be falling apart and all the old forces of dissension are reappearing. We are witnessing a momentous historical change.

And what if the clergy were to appeal to the army: 'Brothers, it is anti-God to use your weapons against the people'? Would the army hold? Or would it sweep away its own officers? I think it could. Then all would be over in a night, with terrible retribution to follow.

However tomorrow I suppose I will slip back into thinking it will all sort itself out: that they will keep a reduced Shah, and that the mullahs will be bought off. But my bones tell me there is some fearsome Islam on the warpath that has not been seen for generations.

Riots and Military Government

All hell broke loose on 5 November as gangs of rioters bent on arson smashed and burned central Tehran. The British Embassy was put to the torch. The authorities were nowhere to be seen and it is widely suspected that some of the incidents were inspired by the army or Savak in an attempt to force the Shah's hand to bring in a tough military government. He had been observed consulting 'liberal' alternatives to the prime minister.

On 6 November, Sharif-Emami resigned and a military government under General Azhari was installed. Bafflingly the expected hard-line crackdown then failed to materialise, though arrests of some of the old trusties began, not least of the former prime minister, Amir-Abbas Hoveyda; and the press was silenced.

The strikes continued unabated and now spread to the oilfields. Inexorably they began to paralyse the whole system. Foreign expatriates who had hoped the storm would pass now began to pull out. The tight curfew affected everyone's lives. Meanwhile Ayatollah Khomeini, from an apple orchard in Neauphle-le-Château in the western suburbs of Paris, held court to a fascinated world press and incited an armed uprising. Opposition politicians began to visit him from Tehran.

Nevertheless an air of anti-climax, of stalemate even, was the dominant mood. Rumours abounded of new political combinations that might be contrived to replace the military government. The unthinkable began to be said at uptown dinner parties: perhaps it would be for the best if the Shah were to go. Sporadic violence continued in Tehran and other cities, spreading to the oil towns of Khuzistan. On 27 November came what proved to be one of the key propaganda coups of the whole revolution: the publication of a list of 177 rich Iranians who had allegedly sent their money out of the country.

Apprehension mounted as to what 'the opposition' (they were not yet referred to as revolutionaries) would attempt to do over the key mourning days of Tassu'a and Ashura on the 9th and 10th of Moharram in December.

THURSDAY, 2ND

I think wisdom is showing through – late in the day and fraught though the situation is. Talked to a man-of-the-people today, very close to the bazaar and the mosque; and to a senior mandarin of government. Both had much the same to say: the people, left to themselves, were not revolutionary but were discontented. The Shah had become too grand, too remote, and was now seen to have been fallible in his management. The people, led by the mosque and with no little support from the intellectuals, wanted to pull him back, but not to overthrow him. They wanted a voice – through parliament or the press or some institution – which they have been denied in order to achieve a balance between autocracy and democracy (automatically accepted as never fully practicable in Iran).

There was no religious revival as such; religious observance among the masses had always been there. The vast majority of people of all classes (save the peasants) would not contemplate living under an 'Islamic' government. There never had been such in Iran, and it was inconceivable to impose it after the advances of the last fifty years.[1] Most of the students screaming in support of Khomeini would loathe it too. It was just that Khomeini was a focus of opposition because of his exile and attractive because he was not a compromiser.

He was clearly the problem. He appeared an obdurate, prejudiced, vengeful, intransigent man – but had now to be taken into full account. The only way to win him back might be by a grand gesture of reconciliation from the Shah. Then his sting could be drawn – if the government nerved itself to a few days of emotional fervour in his favour on his return. But he must not be allowed to bring the whole of society down because of his personal vendetta with the Pahlavis (his father is said to have been killed by Reza Shah, and it is put about that his eldest son died in unexplained circumstances last year).

Broadly the same view is now expressed by many loyalists: why won't the Shah show himself, speak to his people, appeal to his people? He must find the confidence to do so – but it goes against his grain and his aloof style of ruling (a failing which has denied him the people's love), and he is now paying the price.

Again the same praise for the BBC – the Truth, not accessible otherwise. But David Owen has done untold damage to the British name, not so much in standing by the Shah, but in doing so entirely uncritically, linking his support to oil and arms and giving no recognition of the reality of popular discontent and simply slandering 'the opposition' as fanatical. Nobody, nobody, wants military government of any kind, either a generals' government on behalf of the Shah (thought increasingly possible) or a radical one (that is, a coup).

Bad though the present 'fever' (an analogy often used) is – unprecedented indeed even during Mussadeq's days[2] – it is only a psychological purgative that Iran inflicts on itself every generation or so. The therapy, while painful and dangerous, could prove beneficial, some argue. This is the view of the middle-class Establishment, which is now prepared to admit the errors of the past and the Shah's fundamental misjudgements. But, they assure me, don't get alarmed, we will come through 'this difficult patch' (i.e. a reformist not a revolutionary outcome).

I would like to believe it, like to believe it will all sort itself out; like to believe we are just seeing excitable youths out for a rag and not knowing what they are doing; but equally I ask if we are not all still underestimating the forces that have been released and their capacity and wish for the destruction of the whole order?

Nicaragua on the news tonight (such a subject on Iranian TV in itself unprecedented). How near we are to it. We could be only a few weeks away from outright repression and armed struggle here if things are not handled well.

Yet there is hope – at least in an increasingly apprehensive middle class. It seems unthinkable that all this could be swept away. 'It can't be true,' people say. 'Good sense and the compromising Iranian character will prevail.' No doubt this has been said before in history! But I take some heart from the report of the Shah granting an audience to Amini.[3] No one has a good word to say for the latter – not trusted by the army, nor by the Shah, mistrusted by the National Front, rejected by Khomeini. Seen the other way, this is a good recipe for a man who can hold the centre! I thought he was a genuine politician and liberal when he was in power before – and today's newspaper interview reads convincingly. But would he be the Kerensky? And could he calm the people? I believe the risk has to be taken. There is no solution by the other route. Yet he is seventy-three: that is the rub. Fifteen years of political obeisance and there is now no statesman under sixty-five. Only one person has so far mentioned Alikhani[4] – able, attractive, liberal, but tarnished by his acceptance of Princess Ashraf and Alam's patronage. Still lying entirely low.

Among the middle class there is contempt for the mullahs and cynicism about their sincerity. They are only after increased subsidies or restitution of their lands. They are seen as something irrelevant and left behind – and there is complete disbelief that the average educated, modern Iranian could ever acquiesce in living under their rule.

And then one looks down onto the streets. As we talked the familiar thrash of a helicopter passed overhead and against it could be heard the now-familiar chant of a distant mob. Then they appeared – sixty or seventy rampaging students – shinning up buildings in Elizabeth Boulevard and tearing down Pahlavi plaques (roars of triumph when they were thrown down with cries of 'Death to the Shah') and then dashing on to hurl bricks through plate-glass windows. What fun, what giddy excitement!

Or one reads of 200,000 demonstrating in Qom at the behest of the mullahs. Is this going to pass so easily? Is it just a fever? Or – like the IRA – is every argument to reason and good sense going to be rejected so as to press on to revolution itself? It is in the balance, I believe – and this is frightening, not least because of the increasingly vocal hostility towards foreigners.

How short most memories are – if not the Shah's. Reading again the history of the years since 1945, one sees how they are relapsing into the same old paralysis and destructive conflicts that have always held this country back. The hysteria of the people; the conservatism of the clergy; the negativeness, factionalism and indecisiveness of the Majles. The Shah knows all this – he has witnessed it for thirty-seven years. Hence his dejection at seeing it all rise up again and the sense of failure, of hopelessness, at having failed to exorcise it by his reforms. He did get on top of it, he did achieve so much – but then squandered it by *folie de grandeur*. What a tragedy it all is.

As yet one event that has always played a key role in Iranian political events – assassination – has not been used. And it has nearly always been at the hands of the religious. But everyone says things have never been as bad as this before. Reading back though, I wonder? The difference between Mussadeq's times and now is this: his crisis was in part over the failure of the Majles to produce decisions or good sense – and so the Shah took over in order to rule himself. This time it is the failure of that very rule which is the true bitterness for the Shah (no exculpating him), for he knows the only alternative is to go back to the Majles and the mullahs who made a mess of it before – or to the army, or the communists. Iran's dash for true independence is in jeopardy.

SATURDAY, 4TH

A bad day it seems, though I saw not a trace of trouble. Some students rumoured killed outside the university – and the Inter-Continental Hotel definitely beaten up.[5] That's what those helicopters were: they circle over riots like vultures over a kill. One then knows where the trouble is.

Fear again. One detects it straight away as people start ringing one another up just for comfort or to supplement their information. The university is inflamed (even since I was last there). Emotional meetings addressed by released prisoners. The place is in a fever and a fury. One senses they want their own martyrs. Alarming and frightening. It is going to be difficult to calm this down – or even now to shoot it down.

Yet today I drew increasing hope that moves to reconciliation have apparently begun. The Shah is prepared to talk even to Karim Sanjabi (of the National Front).[6] Astonishing, but it must be a move in the right direction. But all so late and under duress. The key is with a combination of the clergy and the National Front – they have discipline, as their great peaceful marches have again demonstrated. Perhaps the students can simply be allowed to sound off while the real moves take place elsewhere.

It snowed in Shemiran for the first time tonight.

SUNDAY, 5TH

It broke today. Quietly to work. Papers full of troubles yesterday which we had not seen. Should I drive past the university today to view? Such is/was one's almost frivolous attitude; but by early afternoon it had changed from spectator sport to drastic involvement. I have felt vaguely immoral for weeks in taking a vicarious enjoyment – yes – in the unfolding drama. Now came the reckoning: real personal fear, suddenly. Real remorse that one had not heeded the danger signals. We have talked, talked and scarcely acted. Now with a rush it is on us ...

A lunch of illusory calm and comfort in the Imperial Club.[7] Driving back it was soon obvious something was wrong: cars streaming out of town with their headlights on, honking their horns. And not smog but rolling smoke ahead. I first smelt it at Abbasabad. By the office, many columns of smoke rising to the south. Fires had been set throughout the central area and the columns of smoke were moving closer. Yet no sign of troops or police. Gangs started running down Karim Khan Zand Avenue.[8] Fires erupted from overturned cars, groups tore down shop fronts. All round was smoke and tongues of flames. Yet people were excited rather than terrified – all so boyish and prankish. Thick smoke towards Ferdowsi Avenue. Yet no sign of helicopters or the sound of firing. Later learnt of the sack and pillage of the British Embassy, and of heavy firing downtown. Looked apocalyptic from the office balcony.

Escaped home, dodging demonstrations, running the gauntlet of burning oil drums thrown in the road and having excited youngsters banging on the roof and windows shouting 'Marg bar Shah' (Death to the Shah) at me and demanding I put my headlights on in sympathy. Elahieh still peaceful. No troops in sight. Hectic ringing all evening. Everyone ringing in. By nine o'clock the stillness of the curfew (reimposed). Everyone ringing – will Sharif-Emami fall tonight? Will the tanks move tonight? Rumours abound: the Shah had left, the air force had mutinied, troops were fraternising with the people in the streets, General Ovaissi had been assassinated.

MONDAY, 6TH

The day after the storm. An hour or two of telephoning around and then off with a mixture of trepidation and adventure to keep a meeting. Elizabeth Boulevard littered with charred vehicles; bank and hotel windows smashed, some scarred with fire.

But the army is back: helicopters again overhead – comforting in a way. As we talked a gang ran shouting down the street, preceded by cars giving warning with headlights on and honking. So like the African wild: the vultures over the kill and the gazelle fleeing before the lion.

Nervous staff left the office as we talked, and then everything was dropped while we listened to the Shah's broadcast on a little transistor. As usual low-key, unemotional, sincere, calm, in that soft, high-pitched voice. Effective – if believed. Certainly calmed the immediate situation. But the action, rather than the words, is the iron fist. Will everyone now shut up and go home with their tails between their legs? Or will they *have* to be shut up as in Indonesia or Chile or Nicaragua? Or will it prove unshut-upable? I fear it cannot be stopped.

A trail of wrecked banks and shops to the spectacular blitz in Karim Khan Zand. The burnt-out Bank Melli tower and the still-smoking pile of bricks and girders that had been the NIGC building and the BMW agency.[9] Knots of people on the streets – who was friend, who was foe? Fine clear afternoon with only occasional columns of new smoke. Distant rattle of guns.

Later visited the embassy – charred and scarred. Terrifying moments – a rampaging, reckless mob and not a whit of help. Suspicions that the whole affair was directed by two or three older men who had stood back and not taken part. Who – Savak? The army itself? Why? The implications are really shaking. By contrast the US Embassy remained closely guarded. As we talked down there, three Chieftain tanks[10] thundered and clattered past on their way to the bazaar area. All Israeli families were evacuated today by military airlift. We hesitate and debate.

Many had been relieved – my tea boy for one – to hear the Shah. 'Who else have we?' they ask. I wonder if he has been so shocked and depressed as people say? Has he been biding his time all the way through but putting up a show of talking to politicians? I don't believe so. I think this has been forced on him.

Military government was announced later in the day.

TUESDAY, 7TH

First full day under army rule. Soon clear there is no real confidence. Order on the streets, yes, and only sounds of some distant mopping-up operations. Everyone sweeping up debris and broken glass and beginning the process of repair.

Incredible scenes outside the petrol stations. Queues and queues of cars, milling crowds, with police and armed troops trying to keep some order. Four to five hours to get a tank full. Everyone ringing everyone as is now the habit. Evacuation or not? I am still stunned by the realisation of what was perpetrated at the embassy. How near this was to an Abadan cinema disaster. How the rioters were so purposeful and under some form of control. Of the eighteen-year-olds tearing up the visitors' book and systematically smashing tables, cups – while staff looked on with fury and frustration. We were paid off for David Owen and, above all, for the BBC. The Americans on the contrary were closely guarded. The French were not touched, presumably because of the likely effect on Khomeini. The worst moment in the British Embassy sacking was when fierce rioters tore the hosepipes out of the hands of staff in order to let the building burn.

In the afternoon the first report of arrests. And of General Khademi's[11] murder or suicide. The axe is falling. There feels to be nothing but violence and retribution ahead. I cannot feel the prospect of peace, no matter what weight those armed forces have.

One rumour, that Dr Amini had succeeded in forming a government, including the National Front, and that this had been approved by the Shah; but that Khomeini was refusing to give it his support. At this Amini said there was no point in continuing, as Khomeini alone carried the streets. So there was no alternative but to turn to the generals.

The voyeurism has now stopped and one is faced with disagreeable decisions on staying put entirely or beginning to pull up roots.

WEDNESDAY, 8TH

Hard to judge things without, above all, local newspapers (that brief blaze of freedom is being snuffed out and no doubt the usual propaganda sheets will soon appear). But clearly the next week or two are touch-and-go for the authority and effectiveness of this military government. I have no doubt that street disorders are over. Isolated acts of sabotage and terrorism are all that will be able to occur – and even on these, people may bide their time to see which way things are going to move. No, the real weapon of dissent will continue to be the strikes. If irreconcilable, even when confronted with force, then the game will soon be up. Two weeks? Three?

So what will the military government do? Restore law and order and services (the opposite side of the coin to strikes). But then? Deliver the heads people are calling for. Hence the arrests that began yesterday (poor, old gentleman Khademi murdered and Iraj Vahidi,[12] so cheerful and almost carefree only last Wednesday, arrested). Hoveyda to follow today or tomorrow. Then must come attempts to placate the main themes of discontent: and one of these is that there are too many foreigners. Under law and order, there will be no attacks on foreigners, but no doubt a hundred obstacles and much administrative aggro will be put in their way. Droves of them are already leaving and the airlines are overwhelmed. Now all is paralysed with the progressive breakdown of the telex and computer systems. We are beginning to be beleaguered – in a modern state.

But where, after these initial moves, does the military government go? Will the Shah use it simply to hold the line? Or are political moves going on to try to construct an acceptable civilian government? Yet any combination is subject to Khomeini's veto – and he is clearly going to withhold this until the country becomes ungovernable and the regime fails, as powerless to operate. These are the hopeful and the hopeless scenarios.

Meanwhile the town looks like the aftermath of an air raid in the Blitz, with shopkeepers and bank clerks sweeping up the broken glass (or in some cases already installing new panes). The traffic is light, and the scarred asphalt on roads still betrays where the pyres of furniture and papers burned. Few troops are to be seen or helicopters to be heard, but the British Embassy has a brave show of three armoured cars outside it – if ever a case of the stable door and bolted horse.

I called on the head of the foreign exchange department of one of the banks that had been burnt. He and his staff had been left with only scattered files and papers. There they were, sitting on the floor out in his makeshift office, trying to sort out charred and crumpled documents and preparing telexes for banks abroad to ask them what payments or transfers were due so that they could begin to reconstitute their records. Was one to laugh or cry?

Then the hard personal political news comes in. Of Hoveyda, of Khademi – and the rumour that Ansari[13] has fled by Cessna with a false passport to Turkey (the justification these developments provide for having had a nest-egg abroad after all).

THURSDAY, 9TH

The day after the arrests. The day before Eid-e Ghorban (the Feast of Sacrifice). The day or two after people begin moving round town again and putting the legion of stories about Saturday and Sunday into a coherent picture.

For us, emerging from it all, is the realisation of the calculated but highly controlled burning of the British Embassy. For every event there are instantly three versions: the truth (probably) first, then the opposition's theory, and finally the regime's statement. Take poor General Khademi's death. I first learnt he had taken his own life when they had come to arrest him. Knowing the old-school gentleman that he was, honourable, sensitive, I frankly believe this. But the regime has him shot down by opposition guerrillas who broke into his house. And the opposition has him shot 'resisting arrest' by the officials who came to arrest him so as to silence him.

So it is with everything. Can professional soldiers unversed in politics, much less economics, hope to master a highly charged, passionately bitter situation such as this? Or is it the last hours with the last card played? Already, unnerving stories of what is to happen on Saturday (there is always a 'day' just ahead of us) when tens of thousands are veritably to offer themselves as sacrifice.

One resists alarm, resists the rumour, resists hasty action, but fear and apprehension suddenly bear in on one. What reason has one to think it will work out? Why should these generals succeed at all? Why should such a desperate throw work? Why should people not see through this duplicity as they have seen through every other one?

I rode with the proverbial taxi driver tonight. Three themes: what satisfaction did the people get from the arrest of Hoveyda and Nassiri and their like? They almost (not quite) sympathised with them – after all they had only carried out their master's orders. He, the Shah, was the one responsible. It was him, personally. He had never been the man his father had been. Then the simple uneducated Iranians had needed a tough, plain-spoken autocrat who meant what he said; but 'this one' never said anything he meant – and he was dealing with educated men, doctors, engineers. That is why all confidence and trust had been lost. Then on Islam. The government was smearing Islam, smearing Khomeini. He and his colleagues wanted a sensible, moderate Islam – they were not fanatics. They didn't want to go back a hundred years. Yes, they wanted indecent cinemas restrained; yes, they wanted women to be discreet in dress; yes, they wanted the Qur'an and the Islamic law reasonably observed. But they were painted by the authorities as obscurantist fanatics for thinking thus. All this from my taxi driver in plain, forceful language as he wended and twisted his way through the traffic. A good man, I would judge.

And he is convinced of the hand of Savak in the burning of the embassy (or the Irano-British Bank, or British Airways for that matter). He takes it as self-evident, even to the two allegedly Savak officers in plain clothes who directed the affair (perfect match with the story as told by the embassy people of two men, of a different stamp to the rioters, who stood back but were regularly consulted by them).

The total duplicity and moral confusion of Iran. They even deceive and baffle one another! But not all. Can they ever change? A plague on them all – and yet able to be so agreeable and attractive.

No papers for days – even the taxi driver remarked on it. And the radio is completely controlled again. The brief 'flowering' (it was, by Jove) is over. Now the harassment of foreign correspondents begins. The borders are all but closed. The shutters are coming down. Why is H.I.M. worried? Let him relax behind the new authority.

The total cynicism of this belief in 'negative collusion'. Not that the anti-Shah rioters and the pro-Shah forces are working together – no. But where the latter want to register their displeasure, or their support, it is made clear. So the rioters perceive where is free-for-all, where no-go, and act accordingly. Then both achieve their different objectives – and the British get clobbered from either side.

No press. Suddenly one is out of touch, and what could be happening in the dark out there is unknown. The riots were in Zanjan today, they say.

FRIDAY, 10TH

Talked to my touchstone, my gardener, Goudarzi, who is a good man and a faithful member of his local Shi'a 'chapel'. He and his son (a bus driver) and his other son (a conscript soldier) have no doubt about the moderation and good sense of their cause. They believe (like that taxi driver) that Islam and Ayatollah Khomeini are being given a bad name by 'them'. They say that all Khomeini – who is at one with his fellow clergymen and no fanatic – wants is the release of prisoners unjustly imprisoned, his own return to 'rule' if necessary, and the restoration of a decent social order based on Islam. Goudarzi vehemently denies that any religious leader wants to see burning or killing. This was done by 'them' and – unfortunately – the Shah. People were confused and baffled as to why so many were being killed. In every town in the country there was mourning. Eleven shot in his own town of Borujerd. The soldiers were part of the people, their own; but duty demanded that they shoot if they were ordered to. They did not like nor understand it, but they were told to do so by their superiors when they saw rioters disturbing the peace. But who was ordering them to do this?

Iranians were not against foreigners as such – why should they be? Except for the Americans who supported the Shah. But the English (who were friends of Khomeini) and the French (who were sheltering Khomeini) and even the Russians, were not enemies. Simple fellow that Goudarzi is – though astonishingly well-informed from his local conventicle – he says that the people are relieved the army has brought back order; and they believe that this will give time to form a 'good' government. Then all will be well. They do not expect much of it but it will not be thieving like the last one.

He extended an invitation that I should join him, as I did two years ago, with his friends in his chapel on the mourning days of Ashura.[14] His friends had asked where I had been last year (abroad in fact) and had invited me again this year. If I was together with him, what reason had I to fear? And I believe him. He would see that no harm befell us in our house or in our garden.

Shortly afterwards I went to a sadly constrained Remembrance Day service at the war graves cemetery in Qolhak, at the embassy. Constrained because it was thought best that we offer no provocation by singing Christian hymns. I wonder? Was this necessary? Made one feel a stranger needing to hide one's own faith. Who said it was necessary?

A good feature of the crisis is the 'wartime' camaraderie. We call on friends as friends rather than meeting in parties. When things are tense (or felt to be) we ring one another up just to chat, just to be in touch. If the telephone workers were to strike, it would be the greatest blow to expatriate morale.

It is said the Shah has pulled out of his despair and indecisiveness; but it is still not clear whether he is master of his officers or they of him – law-and-order rather than political animals though one supposes them to be. Certainly I find it hard to see him as the cynical Machiavelli who could deliberately turn a blind eye to the sacking of the British Embassy while regularly talking to the ambassador. If the decision was made not to strive officiously to keep it safe, I see it more at the hands of senior officers who had the immediate security problems to face and were most likely to resent the BBC's alleged subversiveness.

To me all depends on the next two weeks and whether the strikes abate or not. If they do not, authority and this regime cannot survive. And then the prospect is frightening. Fear, real fear, returns, for we are unlikely to see a controlled transition to constitutional government.

There is a poison in the system now, a viciousness, a destructiveness. In short, a furious revolutionary feeling. So many of the leaders seem paralysed, lacking in confidence, sitting glumly at their desks, or pacing the floor nervously. There is such a sheer weight of difficulties to overcome, and with the mass of the people against them to hinder solutions.

SATURDAY, 11TH (EID-E GHORBAN)

This absence of newspapers doesn't help. The new government is virtually unknown to any of us. No one wanted or wants a military government. In terms of law and order what can they do that martial law could not do? And any suggestion that they can handle the economy or society better is nonsense. How can they begin to tackle the expiry of business confidence and the flight of Iranians and expatriates alike, now gathering force, from the stricken ship (or so one feels it, half dismasted, running out of fuel, and wallowing in a becalmed sea between storms)?

First continuous all-night rain last night – at least there will be skiing[15] in a week or two! Dank, chilly and raining all day.

Further thoughts on the way ahead: the worst visible scenario is that the strikes continue and the snarl-up of commercial and private life worsens. The generals cannot shoot – though they are trying to bully – people back to work. Shoot some ringleaders? They would then be shown to be helpless and would have to turn to a political alternative – and accept the strikers' political demands (free all prisoners – bring back Khomeini – hence out with the Shah – and install a just Islamic order). We will know in the next two weeks.

If they look like succeeding, then the opposition can play its last card: a direct call by the religious leaders to the armed forces not to fight against 'the people'. This could be dangerous as the present situation is held only by the barrel of the gun and the solidarity of the men behind it. Dare the clergy actually do this – a truly revolutionary act? I have little doubt they would get a response – and if the army breaks, it will break suddenly. It could mean a coup of middle-rank officers against the generals. If successful, they would then turn to the popular forces. I fear that Khomeini and his followers, and the National Front, are determined to see this through to the end and believe that the tide is in their favour. If they weaken, the momentum will be lost, and the millions of fence-sitters will turn back to the authorities. One senses an irresistible force, and desperate measures to hold it, having for so long failed to understand it.

At last I have a fairly convincing picture of the events at the embassy. Rioters – perhaps fifty, turning from sacking the Bank Melli opposite and burning carpets from the Government Carpet Emporium in the street – started to hurl stones at the office block. There was no response. Emboldened, they wrenched off the north gate and poured in. Stones now from all sides. One party set the conference hall alight and hurled a firebomb into the first-floor Commercial Registry. This blaze lit the fuel storage tanks on the north wall and smoke poured into the occupied building. Another group went to the gatehouse and found a load of full butane gas cylinders which by chance had just been delivered. With these they fired and destroyed the gatehouse and the telephone exchange in the main building. Madcaps among them began dragging more cylinders into the reception area.

It must have been terrifying. Some members of staff sought to repel boarders who were mounting the stairs; one of these[16] fortunately understood Persian and heard a rioter shout, 'Get the people out. We only want to burn the building, not harm people.' With difficulty all the staff were got out. Then the gas cylinders went in, but not before one man with a hammer systematically destroyed every object on the ground floor. Somehow there was a restraint in defence, and in attack – exercised by certain individuals standing back in the garden and directing affairs.

Up to now there had been no police evident and no army (400–500 yards away). With the building burning, a troop of soldiers did drive up and the rioters fled; but after making apparent calls for reinforcements, the troops drove off. In the lull, staff began training hydrants and hoses on to the main blaze. Then came a much more hostile mob who tore the hoses out of their hands and cut them: the building had to burn. The staff retreated into the centre of the compound and only this prevented a rampage throughout the garden to destroy the private houses. The fire engine arrived three hours after the trouble had begun.

A late call to a senior commander elicited a response to the effect, 'We had much else to do besides look after you. And what better can you expect after David Owen and the BBC?' I attribute it to the army and not to the Shah in person. A clear sign of who wears the boot (Hoveyda's arrest was also said not to have been approved by the Shah).

BBC News says Sanjabi came back from Paris last night and at the airport said that he and Khomeini were of one mind. He then called on the strikers to continue. I'll bet he's inside tomorrow.

It's disconcertingly like Kenya after independence, only in fast time.[17] A strike, or people leaving, cuts off life support services from this company or that institution and suddenly each is shown to be exposed and vulnerable. Wives and children, and many men, are leaving in increasing numbers. On many projects, work could not have continued in any case because equipment or materials were held up in the ports by strikes. It is all expiring on its feet in front of one's eyes. Modern Iran cannot be maintained (or developed further) without these men, at least in the short term.

Announced tonight: Sanjabi arrested. So this *is* the mailed fist. Now there is open confrontation. The rule of force outright. If the inevitable protest is weak, if the strikes peter out, then we have years of military dictatorship. If Khomeini challenges then the test will be on.

What has been happening in the blanket silence of the past few days? Many reports of machine gun fire and isolated shots. Could there have been a widespread liquidation of the ringleaders? When the hard-core prisoners were released recently as a gesture, Iranians said they doubted if the main ones would still be alive in a few weeks (car accidents, etcetera). In the silence of the last few days could all this have been done?

SUNDAY, 12TH

A quiet day but a feeling of emptiness without any news – no local papers, no foreign papers, thinnest radio news as if nothing untoward was happening. Hence we all listen to the BBC.

But one interesting conversation with a young middle-level official: 'This is now a naked power struggle between Khomeini and' – beckoning disrespectfully with his thumb to the inevitable portrait on the wall – 'that guy.' All the rest, he said – 'even Sanjabi – was political manoeuvring and place-seeking'. He had no doubt Khomeini – now the unchallenged Islamic leader over such others as Shariatmadari (whose radical resolution he appeared to doubt) – would not relent, but indeed would have to turn more and more to his real source of power: Islamic solidarity. If he called on the faithful to strike, they would strike (signs of a power workers' strike developing today). What of the army, full of good

Muslims? If he appealed to them not to fight, they would not. But the present was the first, the negative, stage; the second was if necessary to summon his own people to take up arms. This was the positive stage. And make no mistake, the arms were there but not used yet. All this gratuitously (he even initiated the conversation after business had been completed), from a plain, fairly lowly public official.

My own pet theory is that the military will soon begin to get used to power and that they must to some extent have overridden the Shah to achieve it. He is no longer eight feet tall to them. Among them will be two or three officers who enjoy power and are competent (Ovaissi? Gharabaghi?)[18] and may come to see that the Shah has become a liability given popular sentiment. Nevertheless, they want him as a symbol of legitimacy and continuity. Hence, over the next few months he, disappointed, will come to take more and more of a back seat.

And furthermore these officers are close to the people, close to the mosque, and will bend policies to achieve a consensus. And yet ... and yet, his personality is so strong. Not in an overbearing, autocratic way like his father (who had to bend in the end) but in an authoritative, sad, tragic, even moving sort of way. In the way of someone, still apparently young, who has yet been there so long. I can never see him as corrupt and cruel (self-deceiving and therefore deceiving others, yes; weak and indecisive, yes) in the way the enemy wants to cast him. But nor was Hoveyda.

In the expatriate community there is little confidence. Wives and children are going home in droves. Schools are closed, supermarkets half-empty. The men wait behind: even some of them are being pulled out. Whole companies are pulling off the job. Many never loved Iran and are saying good riddance. The whole disliked, pervasive foreign presence is vanishing in front of one's eyes. Thus one of the opposition's prime objectives is being achieved willy-nilly. Yet with renewed stability and wealth, they will all come flooding back – but more charily this time. This flight of the foreigners must have a profound effect on Iranian attitudes – a loss of respect, a confirmation of the belief that they were only here to make their pile and be off. The household packers and truckers are doing a roaring if short-lived trade in personal effects. The Great Retreat is on.

MONDAY, 13TH

Everyone is fearful of the force and revenge of Islam. How quickly from almost nowhere it has come to displace the traditional bogey of the liberals and the Left. Yet any reading of Iranian history should have warned that it, the mosque, could not be overlooked as a power in the land.

The strikes seem to be giving way only slowly, if at all. Petrol is back in the pumps but is said to be only winter reserve stocks (typical rumour – everything has to be given a sour twist). Iranair is flying again and some mail is getting through.

One senior Iranian banker commented that the Shah wouldn't be able to drop the generals if he wanted to. They would hang on to save their own skins having just witnessed what he did to Hoveyda and co. when they stood down. The banker thought that at some point the generals might act against the Shah in order to satisfy public opinion and then put their weight behind a government with some more popular basis.

The belief in the official inspiration and supervision of last week's riots is firmly and widely held, even among the intelligentsia. One man commented that it reminded him of the paid squads of General Zahedi's[19] counter-coup in 1953: educated ringleaders and young thugs. They were not students. No arrests were made on the day of the burning of the embassy (referred to among all the British now as Guy Fawkes Day – which it was actually!) and no one was killed.

I now know of two good men (civilians) who have been asked to take office and who have refused. Hence the government is driven back on ancients or third-raters. A sense of paralysis, stalemate, of waiting for the blow.

TUESDAY, 14TH

Tug o' war on strikes. Government seem to be gaining ground on points – but so little news to go on. People are exhausted by rumours. One must resist the temptation to spread them – aggravates the situation. Burst of trouble down by the bazaar (as seen from my office), with helicopters like wasps nosing around some fires. In the midst of it two squadrons of twelve F-14s in formation wheeled over the city as if practising for a display. Were they? Or was it a show of force?

Some banks are not honouring cheques in full. Nor can banks process promissory notes as the Ministry of Justice is on strike. Is the system seizing up? Or are these just passing dislocations? Certainly irreversible damage is being done to domestic and international business confidence. Iran cannot be looked on in the same way again for years at least – even if all is solved tomorrow.

Ah, for those happy orderly prosperous days of the sixties! Lunch with the great planner of that time.[20] The fatal decision was in 1972 to go for broke after the first oil price rise. He attributes it to Ansari first, then Hoveyda and not entirely to the Shah. He believes the Shah is regaining confidence – hence the four civilian ministers. Interesting that the generals (save the PM) are called not ministers but 'supervisors'. There never was an 'Amini government' in prospect. No one would agree to work with anyone else. The National Front politicians are nice men, but totally inexperienced in government or high politics. The good technocrats are refusing to be drafted – some are even being threatened with exposure of past misdeeds if they withhold their services. So the generals will have to do it themselves. Bad sign that the twelve new provincial governors are all old hacks – no one else will serve. (All comments by my economist friend.)

The main hope must be that authority, no matter how crude, will hold – and the opposition will finally get fed up and will shirk the big challenge. Ahead lies economic disruption, however. Industrialists say their labour deserved increases and they will just have to absorb costs ... and even believe they can!

With many there is despair. They almost seem to want things to get worse. From excitement? Or a death wish? Which is what – a general feeling of guilt that only disaster can expunge? Many recognise that this is almost entirely a self-inflicted wound springing from Iranian arrogance, a conceit, over-confidence and unwillingness to think ahead. *Dorost misheh* ('It'll all come right'), that great Iranian comforter – but sometimes it doesn't. And it all goes back to that second cursed oil price rise, whose excessiveness was a result in part of Iranian arrogance, pride, always knowing best and scorning any adviser's counsel as timid or self-interested.

The Shah seems locked into his own narrow circle of trusties. He threw aside some of the best men – men with independent minds and international reputations – in the early 1970s and now no one will come, fearing also the fate of those who have served in the last few years (Mahdavi,[21] Vahidi, Rowhani, Hoveyda, to name but a few used – or misused – and then discarded).

One asks if the regime deserves to succeed after all this? One feels it does not: and certainly if one was in a democracy the government would be out on its ear at the next election. But here is the awful problem posed by autocracy: the alternative is almost always worse, if only because of the repressed bitterness and frustration. So one clings to what one has, hoping it will change (which it won't and probably can't) until it is finally swept away in some appalling revolution.

Nobody here – not just I – can make up their minds which it is to be. We all vacillate from day to day between hope and despair (and the latter term really would be justified). The hatred and passion and discontent in the people is terrifying – not just the typically radical students. It is easy to forget, of course, that most of the middle or junior officials one meets were students abroad themselves a few years back where they were radicalised for a time. That process has gone on for twenty years or more – and they are to be found at every level.

WEDNESDAY, 15TH

The mood changed today. People have begun to tire of hoping. And with newspapers relying only on rumour and gossip, the hope of the smack of firm government begins to ebb. Both *Time* and the *Economist* came on the bookstalls showing that well-known face (the Shah's) on a poster curling up in flames (contrived or real?) in the street. It was meant to be symbolic and could prove to be so.

I myself believe this military government is the last throw and is no solution. It is a government hated by most, not enjoying the confidence of the rest and with a great popular movement against it. No one knows it. It is coming to seem a twilight period. To match my stories of desperate attempts to get good men to serve, I hear that the new Minister of Finance, 36-year-old Hassan-Ali Mehran,[22] refused the post (he was already in the government). Only when a high-ranking officer prevailed upon his family did he perforce have to agree.

And it was a day when the consequences of last week's destruction came home to roost. The banking system has begun to seize up. Cheques are not honoured, or only in part. The smaller banks begin to look vulnerable. Harsh new exchange controls have been applied. One has a feeling of the whole elaborate engine slowly coming to halt, with steam spurting from every crack.

Meanwhile, somewhere out there is the army. As anticipated, the hard man one hears most of is Ovaissi – ex-Chief of the Imperial Guard (and therefore aware of everything about the Shah) and Head of the Gendarmerie. Typical story about his alleged death. The body was taken to Qom. The mullahs refused it burial and even tugged the beard of the corpse to see if it was false. When clear that the body was not Ovaissi's ('the Butcher of Jaleh'), they still advised its return to Tehran lest people desecrated the grave just in case it was him after all!

So many conflicting stories about the strikes. Tales of intimidation by the army in the oilfields by means of threats of eviction from staff housing. Effective by all accounts. But then rumours of a selective power-workers' strike in Tehran (no sign of it yet). And how the chairman of NPC (the petrochemical company)[23] visited his main plant in an army helicopter and was hardly accorded a hearing. The strikers claimed not to know who he was.

Talk of disputes in the army and the elimination of officers less than firm (I really wonder). Certainly a realisation that the opposition, if it has weapons, has not employed them yet. Does it have them? Is it waiting for its moment? Again, all rather dramatised.

Disrespectful talk of the Shah: *mardike* (that bloke) is how he is said to be commonly referred to. Talk of the French moving Khomeini on from Paris, and then of consequent retribution against the French here. Fear, fear of Moharram, of Ashura (11 December). But one solid thing, though he too again dramatises: a leading industrialist reporting a 70 per cent drop in sales due to the closed bazaar and shops. He fears he cannot meet his commitments by next week – and he heads one of the major groups.

To end on a crisis story, a typical Rashti tale:[24] five minutes before curfew Hassan manages to reach his house. He goes upstairs and finds a stranger in bed with his wife. Quietly he closes the door, goes downstairs and lets himself out into the street where he is immediately arrested for breaking the curfew. 'Surely, you knew?' demands the soldier. 'Well,' says Hassan, 'I also knew it was unlawful to have an assembly of more than two in a house, so I thought I'd better get out!'

At a party this evening. Then driving back at 8.45 with that unmistakable pre-curfew urgency as cars dash for home. Then the town reverts to the silence of the long night and the control of a few soldiers.

THURSDAY, 16TH

An account of the arrest of Sanjabi. Some thirty to forty journalists were actually crowded together in his drawing room being served with tea and cakes by Mrs Sanjabi while he was busy preparing his notes when General Rahimi[25] of the Imperial Inspectorate came in, asked Sanjabi what he was proposing to say and – on hearing it – politely but firmly asked him to come with him. Poor Mrs Sanjabi then had to handle a bunch of excited and frustrated journalists who fell on her and one another with questions for want of anyone else.

But those I have talked to who are seeing Sanjabi, Forouhar, Bazargan, Matine-Daftary, Lahiji[26] – the National Front leaders – all comment on how elderly many of them are, how 'nice' they all are, but how vague, how lacking in any precise programme or knowledge of the real political world, domestic or international. Nor is it clear what real following they enjoy.

FRIDAY, 17TH

Armed Services Day. Never been celebrated like this before. Squadrons of jets fly past and lines of Chinook helicopters wheel in stately file over the city.

I drove past the university which has been shut since the troubles. The Shah's statue at the entrance that I saw defaced two weeks ago has now been toppled. Some railings are wrecked, and the Bank Omran building is gutted. All the big cinemas nearby are burnt out. The campus is still ringed by troops. One simple Turkoman soldier clutched three carnations wrapped in cellophane between his trigger finger and his automatic. Restless groups of five or six hang about the square. Reza Shah's statue is closely guarded.

A long talk about *jihad* (holy war). This can only strictly be declared against the infidel (unbelievers) and not in a civil situation. And it can only be declared on national soil and by a *marja'-e taghlid* (a 'Source of the Emulation' – a leading Shi'ite divine who has achieved a supreme rank giving him authority over followers who 'emulate' his words and actions). And Khomeini and Shariat-madari are both *marja's* but neither has achieved the unquestioned and universally acclaimed status of the late Ayatollah Borujerdi who died ten or more years ago.

On Moharram, despite the inevitably high religious feelings, I believe the *ulema* (clergy) will do their best to see that all this does not lead to violence which would give spiritual Islam a bad name. But acts of provocation may well occur, and the whole place will inevitably be an emotional tinderbox.

Some more stories, for once about Khomeini. Asked whether he approved of card playing, he replied, 'Not for money.' Well, just for the game, then? 'Yes, provided you take out the Kings and provided the Queens are in *chadors*.'

And one on drink. Asked if he permitted the drinking of whisky, Khomeini snorted emphatically, 'No.' Vodka, then? 'No.' Wine? 'No.' What about gin, then? Pause ... 'I haven't tried that yet.'

A mob in Rasht yelling, 'We don't want the Shah.' One Rashti doesn't join in. The crowd shouts at him to do so. 'Why should I, we *have* a Shah now' (Khomeini, that is).

There are so many conflicting accounts on the strikes. The oilfields are up to 2.7 million barrels a day, but many wells and the refinery are only kept going by senior management staff working round the clock. They cannot keep it up for ever. And those workers that have gone back to work often sit there and do nothing – and draw full pay! It is possible that outside technicians and labour will have to be flown in as blacklegs.

What is the position of the senior officers? There are eight of them, of whom I bet Ovaissi and Gharabaghi are the hard men. Will they become a power to themselves? I can't see it in personal terms. But what if the Shah wants to do things that they disapprove of? I believe they can stop – and probably have stopped – him. Or if they want to do things he disapproves of? Same again. Could they come to think that he in his person is an obstacle and suggest that he leave and hand over to a constitutional monarch of a son, untainted except by name? In this way they might preserve the dynasty and the monarchy. Must be a thought in several minds.

Foreign exchange panic tomorrow as the new regulations really hit people and the system. And a shock that the rial will have depreciated against the dollar, not vice versa as many blandly expected!

Inevitable but still ominous news tonight: special tribunals are to be set up to try former ministers speedily. Is it going to be like Turkey all over again when Adnan Menderes went incredulously to the gallows?[27] Turkey was then locked into its still-persisting stalemate of conservative versus progressive forces – with little progress as a result. That has always been Iran's prospect, and the Shah knows it. The awful pessimism that comes out of recent press interviews with the Shah is borne out by friends (save one) who have had recent contact with him. 'Cross fingers,' he said to one. To another, 'I cannot see my way ahead.' Grim-faced, dejected, half-stunned. Hence the long pauses and silences that every interviewer remarks on.

It is gripping to watch. Then fear seizes one and the nastiness of personal anxiety. One feels on the edge of momentous historical events. One's intuitions, all past parallels, say that the game is up. It is desperate, last-throw, backs-to-the-wall stuff.

SATURDAY, 18TH

A political period again. Many contrary strains. Quiet talk of a new political composition being worked out under the shelter of army rule. Of Shapour Bakhtiar (the National Front leader I have always heard best of, and younger – only a mere sixty or so)[28] and of Bazargan treating with Amini and, through him, the Shah. Of Amini or old Entezam[29] as PM. If this is really happening, then there is still some hope.

Yet today I had a senior managing director of a government agency telling me, with growing frankness, that former ministers were not enough: the surgery had to be more drastic. The Shah couldn't change. He was now unacceptable to the people. The people wanted so little; they could never learn democratic methods and compromise unless they had a chance to practise them. He thought that every concession had been a month or two too late, and each further delay polarised the problem still further. Soon armed revolt would take over, not merely unarmed demonstrations. The Shah had to go to avert this.

Seems no doubt at all that Houshang Ansari has gone; has allegedly had a reccurrence of heart strain and is most unlikely to come back. Sharif-Emami and even General Djam (everyone's favourite compromise figure) are mentioned to replace him at the oil company. I guess it will be the former. And also true that old gentleman Khademi was shot down by gunmen and did not commit suicide. Odd: he must have had less to reveal than some others. Some say he helped some offenders to escape by air and evade the net; and he then had high displeasure visited on him (not in character for either). And of course he was a leading Baha'i.[30] No one, but no one, subscribes to the thesis that these generals could feel their oats, learn to like the job and come to think they could do without the Shah. They are too personally loyal and in no way politicians. Azhari,[31] Gharabaghi and old war horse Azimi are most often mentioned (not Ovaissi – how odd). H.I.M. is said to be recovering some of his morale, buoyed up by ringing personal support from Carter and even by direct assurances from Brezhnev – as I have always supposed would be the case.

Where does this balance lie? All history and most parallels suggest we are on the edge of a great and irreversible upheaval, a revolution. The capacity, the passion is certainly there. The calming thought that all this can be 'managed', and on the whole by the same people who got us into it, is a short-term illusion. I vary from day to day, indeed from morning to evening, the former raising fresh hopes while the silent, lonely (if quite contented) hours of the curfew revive one's fears and apprehensions that a great force has been let loose, even if its visible manifestations are cheeky, vicious youths seething with hostility, and an implacable, unshakeable old priest.

One can now often feel that same tension in the streets – people on the edge of hostility, or deliberately rough or rude. Their looks, the deliberate jostling, particularly near the traditional bazaars, as Judy my wife is increasingly experiencing.

Now I see through the ruse of the flowers in cellophane on Armed Services Day: a friend told me he had had to contribute huge sums to provide them! In short, it was all arranged. This is what terrifies me: the authorities are still frivolous, still condescending to the people, still believing that they can dupe and fool them. And they do it in dangerous ways by thus borrowing revolutionary gestures and employing them falsely. You see? If at this point they think they can stem the tide by alternately making empty 'opposition' gestures or provoking trouble so as to give the opposition a bad name, this is criminally stupid and no one will believe in them. This little flower episode worries me. They think things can still be fixed and managed – which shows that nothing has changed or can change.

Are the political moves serious then? Or are the people, the National Front, religious leaders, Ali Amini, being bought off? In which case they run the risk that they will be rejected by the people too and we will have an even more revolutionary situation. And this is a seriously frivolous game if, in the course of it, they permit for instance poor Khademi to be murdered, or the British Embassy to be set on fire with people in it; or the Waldorf Hotel. Or the Rex cinema in Abadan? Terrifying thoughts – but where is the evidence to the contrary? Hence one's continued fear that this will yet blow apart, unless the Iranians are a supine lot through and through and will bow their heads when beaten with a stick or be seduced with a carrot no matter how crudely offered.

There are more reports of threatening telephone calls to ex-patriates or crude letters through the post, of roughings up (in Ahwaz) and even of one house firing. Mainly Americans and some British working in defence-related industries.

SUNDAY, 19TH (EID-E GHADIR)[32]

One can still get away from it all. We went off with a group of friends in Range Rovers for an old-style schnapps-and-smoked-salmon picnic in the new snow at 10,000 feet in brilliant sunshine but with the wind like a keening knife. Needless to say there was no sign of any demos up there!

WEDNESDAY, 22ND

A leaden stalemate. No one believes the strikes are over – indeed we have had no telex or international calls for several days and are having to resort to all sorts of subterfuges to get material back to London. And people talk of the bazaar – or of Khomeini directly

– providing support for the strikers, specifically the journalists and printers. Theirs is a straight test of authority, with the Left more prominent among them than elsewhere.

A speech today (to our Irano-British Chamber of Commerce) by Abol-Ghassem Kheradjou (of the IMDBI)[33] which boldly called into question most of the principal themes of economic policy of the last fifteen years. No name was mentioned, but the criticism was wide-ranging and specific – and public. Quite unthinkable that such things could have been said three months ago and the man survive a week in his job. Kheradjou is detached enough, and bold enough to say it (and canny, for who knows where the tide is running – yet he is too cynical to be ambitious). He stated the four new themes: small is beautiful; an emphasis on agriculture; on nationalism, with a bias against foreign participation; and on consultation not dictation.

We are watching the dismantling of the monarchy. The great inviolate Pahlavi Foundation[34] is being dismembered. Untouchables like Bank Omran are being spoken of as mortal – only too mortal with a 20 per cent loss of deposits – by their own professional executives. It is dying on its feet.

There seems to be truth in the disaffection of certain army units in the 5 November disturbances – and this led to peaks of revolutionary fervour. If I still beg leave to doubt it, I am asked to look at BBC TV or ITN who filmed it (in many ways those abroad know more than we do here!).

THURSDAY, 23RD

Some analogies come to mind: the optimists say this is only 'a fever' that will pass. But could it not equally be a cancer? And another: the Iranians early adopted chess from India. We are certainly in a stalemate. Can they now get to a checkmate (*shahmat* in Persian – 'the King is blocked')?

Change of tack from Brezhnev at last. The Russians too must have seen how shaky and insoluble the situation looks and are preparing their ground in case it breaks up. But I still don't believe that they are presently fomenting it. Nevertheless a bass note to the shrill pipes here which reminds one how this could escalate.

Superficially things seem more solid. General Azhari[35] made a good impression on the box. Sounded quite a politician – much more confident and frank than one would ever have expected. My taxi driver today told me people had liked it and were prepared to believe his words – something, he said, they had learnt never to do from previous governments or, above all, from the Shah.

I pray the authorities allow a fairly free expression on Ashura.[36] There is talk of curfew at 7 p.m., and even of a drastic twenty-four-hour curfew for the three principal days. (Friends are already planning, in wartime spirit, to stay at one house and have continuous parties.) But it will surely be folly to attempt to bottle this up. Left to itself it is unlikely to become political. Contained, it will lead to anger and then violence. God forbid that the 'government' try any provocation to smear the faithful.

A rhyme doing the rounds. It again features the hapless yet versatile Rashtis:

> We are men of Rasht (*Ma mardoman-e Rasht-im*)
> We have offered up our lives (*az jan-e khod gozashtim*)
> Written in mercurochrome (*ba merkurokrom neveshtim*)
> For the Shah ... or for Khomeini! (*ya Shah ... ya Khomeini!*)

I also heard the correct version of my previous Rashti crowd story: a crowd of demonstrators in Rasht is shouting 'We don't want a Shah' (*Ma Shah nemikhahim*). As they turn a corner they find themselves in a cul-de-sac face to face with a squad of armed soldiers. Immediately, to a man, they change their tune to: 'We don't want a shah', meaning Khomeini, a new king, 'because we (already) have the Shah' (*baraye inke ma Shah darim*). In other words, the brave slogans of the Rashtis melt into cowardice at the first show of force.

Another anti-Khomeini crack: when the ayatollah becomes shah his wife will become the Khombanou (the Queen is called the Shahbanou – an invented Pahlavi term).

Worked my way down through a herd of traffic today to the bazaar area. The bazaar had been allowed to open for two days and everyone had gone to buy and sell. If nothing else, these days have demonstrated that, for all the modern streets, the bazaar still dominates the commercial life of Tehran. Still, it was a shock to see such totally naked force down there. One gets used to seeing the khaki-coloured trucks with troops lounging around or sitting chatting inside behind their machine guns, but to see a heavy machine gun hung with loaded bandoliers perched on the first-floor balcony of a house with its French windows open and the gunner training the snout on the bustling crowd below was chastening. Almost every day, I was told in the ministry, there was some shooting down there.

Another light on the crisis in the ministry. It is as if the recent economic drive and the sweeping away of old attitudes of the past twenty years has expired on the spot. Because of a prejudiced, ignorant attack by the Majles on that traditional ogre, foreign loans, the Council of Ministers dared not move to approve the loans before them. The same old suspicions of the foreigner, the same mistrust, the same lack of self-confidence, the same de-fensiveness.

One then sympathises with the Shah. He knew, he knows, what his countrymen are like left to themselves – squabbles, disunity, intrigues, inability to agree on anything. Only a strong autocratic hand can ever get anything done here. I accept this – but then say more's the pity that he didn't use the authority he won for himself more sensibly, more modestly. It was plain *folie de grandeur*, in full plumage, that misled him and has ruined everything. And the

people know it and will not forgive. I am told that he simply
cannot comprehend the tales he hears of rioters calling for his
death and distributing leaflets 'Death to the Shah' (*Marg bar Shah*),
so insulated, so self-involved, so overweening has he become in
that palace atmosphere.

At this very moment the apogee of all adulations of the Shah
has appeared on the bookstalls. Leaves Roloff Beny[37] in the shade.
An Italian 'work' entitled *The Shah/People Revolution is Universal*,
preaching the 'third way' between capitalism and communism as
pioneered by Iran. And the Shah believed this rubbish, encouraged
it and was encouraged by it: was buoyed up by it and sermonised
the world only two years ago! That is why he is in such a state of
shock and disorientation.

Another taxi driver conversation today: the English are good
because the BBC is English and tells the people the truth. Did I
think for a moment that 'the people' attacked the British Embassy
(on 5 November)? Where were the troops that day? Withdrawn so
as to let government thugs, guided by officers in civvies, try to
smear the opposition. (Yes, but 'they' didn't pull down the statue
of the Shah, or wreck the Pahlavi plaques.)

It is typically Iranian that within hours of an event no one is
sure of the truth and there are four 'authentic' explanations: that
even that day (5 November) was thought bogus and a bit of a
prank is extraordinary. There is no one like an Iranian for reading
a conspiracy into everything. Today's taxi man had some weird
theory that the Shah had fomented all the trouble and provoked
the strikers to close the oil wells in order to bring pressure on the
Americans – who had forced him to sell them oil cheaply – to sell
him the arms he wanted more cheaply!

Azhari on TV again, this time addressing the Senate. I must say
in the circumstances he comes over remarkably well. Not the
stern hard soldier of few words, but natural, sincere, simple even,
loquacious (his speech is full of homely analogies), with a nice

modesty and honest bafflement by events. And patently he is a good believing Muslim, well-meaning, rather emotional but devoted to the Shah. Nor did he shirk facing the main issue: the bloodshed by his own troops. But his explanation was either specious or blind. Hard to square this avuncular figure with the armed troops outside. He of course reduced it to simplicities. 'I am not a killer of men; only a killer of enemies.' And the latter are not 'religious people' but 'saboteurs'.

Why did his army stand back on that day? The answer predictably was that 'no one did it'. It was 'someone else' – nevertheless it happened. Won't really convince anyone that Azhari isn't just a nice simple man being used by others, yet he is someone to be reckoned with because he is an upright God-fearing Muslim of principles with an apparent rapport with the people.

As the camera pans the faces in the Majles, they are a study. Here is a man lecturing them from the tribune whom two weeks ago most knew only as a name. And here he is, a comparative stranger, talking away at them, politely but firmly. What are those inscrutable faces thinking? Taking him seriously, other than as a man with force at his command?

SATURDAY, 25TH

It is hopeless to get a proper reading on things without newspapers – it is gossip, rumour, chance serious conversations and 'feel'. The feeling is that the people's attachment to Khomeini is stubborn and that any hope that they are going to be won round by any arrangement dependent on the Shah is wishful thinking. And that is just what the professional classes are busying themselves doing. Of course if no one will face up to it, and 'the people' are not to be won round, then one day there is going to be a big bang. But much of life seems normal and in the bustle of the day one still hopes.

Talk today that four hundred hard-core political prisoners guilty of violence (that is, terrorists) have been released. The Central Bank went on strike and troops are inside the building to guard it.

Perhaps we are seeing a nation dragged back to its own reality and away from a vision which was at the same time a delusion? It's no accident that nations are as they are. They can no more escape their nature than individuals can. They can seem to escape for a time, for better or for worse, but sooner or later the Old Adam, or the Old Angel, redresses the balance. So it's back to the Middle East for Iran and farewell to the Big League adventure.

MONDAY, 27TH

Another rush of trouble. Uproar outside the NIOC building on Saturday.[38] Predictably shots were fired and three people killed in the street (within hours of talk that the military had invaded the building and fired on people in their meetings). So yesterday the NIOC area was sealed off by troops with helicopters overhead. And all about a delegation of workers from the oilfields protesting at pay disputes during the strike. The tension of such incidents immediately communicates itself to the town. One of the surest signs of this is the queues that hurriedly form outside the bread shops.

There is much dispute about some alleged shooting in the shrine at Mashad. One man who was there for Dr Eghbal's[39] anniversary wake swore there had been no violence and that it was all a fabrication by the BBC. But then why did the *ulema* call a one-day strike (which was widely observed) in protest? Or was the reason for that action a rumour too?

As the countdown to Moharram begins, alarmist stories begin the rounds: of 300,000 faithful in Meshed all buying white shrouds (*kafans*) for 'the day', when they will parade in the streets offering themselves as martyrs.

The newspaper dispute seems as insoluble as ever and the

journalists are standing firm that they will not work under censor-ship. Meanwhile the BBC becomes more and more exposed as the only source of news.[40] Therefore the fury at it, or praise of it, becomes even more intense. Much is no doubt in the ear of the listener. Attitudes to the BBC are the best litmus paper to show up the pros and the antis! Whatever the truth, its line reinforces the conviction that the British are behind all these events and have a purpose.

The shadows on the wall about oil are growing sharper. The Consortium – always thought of as British Petroleum plus the British government, whatever the actual shareholding was – had failed to get its way in its talks with NIOC, the argument runs. So in the traditional style it had deliberately agitated the country through its old friends the mullahs in order to weaken the Shah so as to be able to drive a harder bargain. This is a view tenaciously held by many intelligent people.

Another interesting (and significant) political development. Dr Amini was interviewed at length on television. It can only be a deliberate attempt to show him to the people, test the reaction, and – if favourable – let him emerge. Who else is there in the middle? He is of course seen as the American candidate. Also gossip that the CIA have had private contacts with Khomeini in Paris. Another straw in the Amini wind: his son, Iradj, has resigned as ambassador to Tunisia. This removes the only formal Amini link with the existing order – and Iradj himself – for all that he was *chef de cabinet* to Princess Ashraf so recently – is no Establish-ment man (I guess).

A fascinating text is circulating. Genuine or a fabrication? Allegedly a list of those who in the last two months have sent millions of dollars out of the country. A list produced by a dissident official in Central Bank. Yazdani[41] top with 550 million tomans (about £40 million), Ansari with 400 million. A veritable *Who's Who* of Tehran by all accounts.

A similar thing took place two weeks ago when the ex-Savak man Sabeti got out of the country with his wife when on the point of being arrested.[42] Government statements that he was still here were countered by an anonymous letter from an Iranian striker to which was attached a photocopy of Sabeti's ticket (incidentally it is now said that General Khademi, the head of Iranair, was dealt with because he had aided and abetted Sabeti's flight).

As hatches are battened down for Moharram I asked one man, who claims to know, what many army officers were feeling. Growing frustration and impatience, was the reply, that they were still being restrained from dealing with the problem 'firmly'. Soldiers were still being mocked in the streets because people knew they were under orders not to shoot if they could help it (yet why so many shooting incidents then? – every day there is firing, even in Tehran). All very different from talk of the army cracking up and siding with 'the people'.

TUESDAY, 28TH

Things took a provocative turn today with the appearance of this alleged Central Bank list of huge (incredible in fact) sums sent out by 177 named individuals. News of it spread like wildfire in town. Those who were on it were either alarmed or else laughed with scorn at the presumption of it: but people will believe it. Fantastically successful nerve warfare. One of those already out, Houshang Ansari, telephoned from New York as chairman of NIOC and sent a wreath to Dr Eghbal's anniversary in Mashad.

There was a new feeling in town. The traffic jams were worse than ever; the anxious and yet patient crowds once more milled round the petrol stations (most already shut); there was an urgency in the way cars drove; a new surliness in taxi drivers. There is definitely a renewed feeling of something imminent. Then tonight, as if to reinforce the point, all the lights went out at about 7.30.

Stumbling around with candles, deprived of radio and television, driven in on themselves, people began to feel that this simply cannot go on. Something has to give. Will it, or will it have to be fought? If it goes, will there be a great explosion of joy for a few days (yes) to be followed by a new era? Or revenge and discord and decline? Or have we still to grit our teeth and believe that firmness and resolve will see us/them through?

Meanwhile a new social life has been burgeoning. Drinks at 5 p.m. and all off and away by 8.30. Even dinner parties. The usual six-nights-a-week pace of Tehran soon builds up even in this restricted form; but fidgets start at 8.15, there is continual clock-watching at 8.30, and agitated but cheerful leave-taking by 8.40 at the latest so as to reach home in a dash before the 9 p.m. curfew.

In town the subsidence of business life continues. The haemorrhage of funds from the banks is astonishing. Spurred by the dislocation of the branch system and fearful of leaving any funds on account, people are withdrawing cash in notes and keeping it under the mattress or in a safe. The banks are expiring on their feet and Central Bank is having to pump in new funds from their statutory reserves. Companies are going bust, small businesses in the bazaar ruined.

WEDNESDAY, 29TH

Suddenly silence falls. The dash is over – we're home by 8.55. The pace drops. We're all back in our kennels, brooding. A country can't live like this for very long.

In most places the plate glass is in again following 5 November but with it new bars and grilles. All the hope, all the openness is shrinking. The new museums are hostages; many restaurants are shuttered up (and the French Club[43] is therefore even more a meeting ground).

The List has the upper classes in jitters, even though people see it is a fake. There is a revolutionary smell about it – the list for the People's Court. Some are incensed that their honour is impugned; others are livid that they have been missed out, so affecting their status or credit-rating; and others have a nasty feeling down their spines. A highly effective piece of work.

Hard to resist the build-up of pressure, but no one knows quite about what. Who's going to do what? Or who did what? Someone said that they had met National Front people, or Tudeh (communist people) or released prisoners. But who has ever met anyone who has actually burnt a bank? Where have they gone?

The common story of those with gunshot wounds whose parents wouldn't take them to hospital for fear that they would be arrested: so wounds were treated amateurishly at home.

And the next shift of journalists has arrived to feed, as one graphically put it, 'on the carrion of the crisis'.

THURSDAY, 30TH

A typical day in the life of the beleaguered. Rose at 6 a.m. in order to arrive at the garage before anyone else to get a fill of petrol ... the queue was at least a quarter of a mile long and had begun before 5 a.m. Eighty minutes later I got my precious nectar of benzene.

Bridget[44] secured an exit visa today, though having to pay a 'fine' of 10,000 rials (about £80) in order to obtain it because an essential tax clearance had been 'held up for five weeks in a strike'. Clearly it was nevertheless her 'fault' that she didn't have the clearance – hence the fine. Armed with the receipt for the payment, she went to the clerk holding that sacrosanct rubber stamp. 'You want an exit visa?' said he. 'Then I would like some milk powder.' 'But I don't have any,' she wailed. 'No, I know,' he retorted pointedly, 'but the chemist up the road does!'

A meeting today of the British community wardens with the

ambassador, Tony Parsons, in Qolhak.[45] Among his general guidance he said that we had no doubt heard that he was being
transferred (on promotion in fact). Three explanations were doing
the rounds for this, he said: he had been demoted by the Foreign
Office; he had resigned in disgust at the BBC; and, the best, the
BBC had had him sacked!

Azhari has clearly made a good impression on TV, for all that
people are grasping at any straw. Seemed simple and honest and
not dictatorial – everyone's idea of the nice responsible officer
doing his duty. And Amini was well received too, not as the wily
politician but as a man arguing for a commonsense centre position. His son Iradj, now back in town, has everyone in the club
bowing and waving to him, part curiosity, part friendship ... part
reinsurance!

All this is on the positive side but the fear (for me) comes from
the braggadocio of the young toughs all around town. They are
arrogant, rough, breathing violence, menace and irresponsibility
like twenty-year-olds anywhere. The moment, one begins to feel,
is becoming theirs. They have the modern attitude to violence
and the disrespect for elders and foreigners, like the Red Brigades.
One senses their hysteria and viciousness and destructiveness.
Herein lies the fear.

At 7 p.m. the ritual blackout which further intensifies the fren-
etic dash home. For days now from 8.15 onwards no one pays any
attention to the traffic lights; but when there are no lights it's
even worse. Then like rabbits into our holes we all go – and then
straight on to the telephone, cheerfully and breathlessly, to one
another. This crisis is like wartime: it goes on and on and one
learns to adapt to the new life-style.

Expatriates are once more leaving in droves before Moharram.
Private sales notices are stuck on walls or tree trunks (there are
no papers to advertise in). More and more threatening letters and
telephone calls. All jet fuel has run out at Mehrabad airport so

international flights are having to fuel at Athens or Kuwait and only touch down at Tehran.

Khomeini issues threatening calls to action. The next few weeks must decide it for the short term: if he overplays his hand, he could lose momentum and the hardship of striking could begin to tell (though most are reporting for work and then not working, while drawing full pay).

Last race meeting at Farahabad racecourse. Of the season? Or the last race meeting? Melancholy conversation with one man close to the Shah. All the growth of sport and culture was over, blighted by slashed budgets and political opprobrium. Showjumping, the racecourse – with a despairing gesture to the grandeur about him – tennis, even skiing were the obvious victims. All had three flaws: they were for the rich, they had royal patronage, and they were foreign in style. Now everything had to be *mardomi* (popular, in the sense of for 'the people'). Of the new sports of recent years only football looked like surviving; and traditional Iranian wrestling of course. It was to be egalitarian and cheerless. All attempts at excellence and style were becoming suspect.

Hearing this man talk, it dawned on me that to him – so close to power – what he was describing had already happened. Truly we are witnessing a revolution in slow motion. The new ethos, the new style, is seeping through the shell of the old. It is a tide – irresistible. But if it has to happen, let it happen gradually by squeeze, not by crunch.

One feels all that was friendly turning unfriendly; and those that were always hostile to foreigners now daring to show their hostility. It shows from looks, to jostles in the street (to foreign women in particular), to sharper words from people one never expected them from. Having regarded oneself as an accepted part of the country, one comes to feel an alien, an intruder. How the TV is making increasing genuflections to Islam: its discussion programmes, its 'still' inserts (now more frequently of mosques).

10.15 p.m.: SOS telephone call from a friend downtown. Heavy and continuous machine gun fire had broken out around them. Sounds of weird and frightening ululations. Helicopters circling overhead.

Moharram Marches and the Foreigners' Exodus

The pace suddenly quickened. Large-scale demonstrations occurred, now openly Islamic in character. Martial law came to seem almost a dead letter. The overall death toll was put at 1,600 since January. However the great confrontation on Ashura on the 11th, awaited with such apprehension, passed off relatively peacefully amid scenes of mass excitement, now openly anti-Shah.

A general paralysis of the economy and banking system set in. The movement inexorably took hold and extended its reach into the districts and villages. But generally there was a lull after Ashura ... until the gunning down of a senior American oil executive on 23 December. Then the exodus of foreigners really took wing.

In Paris the French did no more than wag a finger at the Ayatollah while he was busy proclaiming 'Blood will triumph over the sword'. The unrest spread among Iranians worldwide: on what was to prove to be his last visit to Washington, the Shah had to face demonstrations while standing alongside President Carter on the White House lawn.

Abol-Hassan Bani-Sadr emerged as a new name among those surrounding Khomeini in Paris. The first public sign of what lay ahead was his article in the New York Times on 11 December in which he wrote of the extent of 'popular support (in Iran) for Islamic precepts and the goal of national independence'.

The only bizarre note of normality in all this was an announcement *from Buckingham Palace on 7 December that the Queen and Prince Philip were to call at Bandar Abbas and Hormoz in HMY Britannia in February. Presumably a vain gesture of support from HMG!*

By the end of the month the effect of the strikes on daily life was beginning to tell, particularly with the imposition of petrol rationing. Meanwhile the endless rumours of new political figures who could be the salvation of it all, such as Gholam-Hussein Sadighi, suddenly became more precise in an unexpected direction: Dr Shapour Bakhtiar, one of the leaders of the opposition National Front.

SATURDAY, 2ND (I MOHARRAM)

A further and definite turn of the screw. People hesitant about coming into town to work after that night of gunfire. Endless trading of stories. My driver's house was in the thick of it in one area. At 10.15 p.m. (the beginning of Moharram) people came out on to the roofs of houses and started shouting *Allah-u Akbar* (God is great). A great commotion began. Other youths ran through the streets shouting 'Death to the Shah'. Troops opened up on the demonstrators and on the houses. With varying intensity firing went on until about 3.30 a.m. The government says seven were killed, but knots of boys carrying bloodstained shoes or shirts are running through the streets shouting 'Three thousand dead, three thousand dead!' They want to be martyrs: to provoke and agitate.

No sooner to work in the morning than a power cut came. Then sporadic shooting, automatic and single-shot, began in the downtown area and gradually moved up towards us. An occasional fire was set. Most people quit the city centre by midday.

A telling story today: a mullah comes to a private house for a family occasion to give a sermon. Seeing a picture of the Shah on the wall he asks the lady of the house to take it down. Under protest she grudgingly complies. While he is talking, she busies herself by cutting out newspaper clips of Khomeini's photograph, puts them in an envelope into which she would normally have put the cash offering for the preacher's services, and gives this to him, sealed, as he leaves. Later he rings to say there must have been some mistake? 'No,' says she, 'there was not. I was sorry that the Shah's portrait appeared to bother you but I couldn't find any banknotes that didn't have it on, so I thought you'd be happier with a picture of Khomeini.' Silence.

The degree of confusion and bewilderment and credulity is alarming. People cannot conceive that they have brought this on themselves: therefore there must be a hidden hand. And the old bogey of oil is growing fast in the rankings as favourite scapegoat. And, of course, where there is oil there also is the hand of the British. Religious elements are another: the British, of course, again. Add one to the other and Khomeini is, QED, a tool of the Consortium.[1] This is a knee-jerk reaction with most Iranians – except the Left, who have other theories.

Sudden darts of nervousness about the Left today. Certain unmistakable signs and jargon that belong only to the Tudeh (communists) – *mardomi* for one ('the People').[2]

The graffiti of *Javid Shah* (Long live the Shah) sprayed on the walls are beginning to fade and a new slogan is supplanting them: *Mohi-ud Din* (Restorer of the Faith) that is, Khomeini.

The effect on the economy is catastrophic. The banking system is virtually paralysed. The whole trading and money system is breaking down. Four banks are said to have failed and only to be supported by the Central Bank (Darioush, Shahryar, Iranians and the great Saderat). Central Bank (Bank-e Markazi) itself is paralysed, while the senior men try to refute that insidious List. The List was cooked up by communist university students and Central Bank strikers. It was rubbish, for most of those on it knew better than to have ever sent money out via the banks when good anonymous black-market foreign exchange was to be had for only a 10 per cent premium.

Outsiders ask why were we all so taken by surprise at events? Because for years the opposition was so silent – cowed, or well-fed? It did not matter: they were silent (other than a few urban guerrillas). This deceived me, deceived world opinion, and above all deceived the Shah himself. It seemed he had it all his own way, apart from a handful of left-wing terrorists easily swatted, and we marvelled at his good luck or, according to some, his good management. He could even lecture the British on their failings (and this is what the Iranians believe the BBC, that is, the British government in disguise, is now getting back at him for).

Midnight. Silence again. Not even any distant shots. A slow rain has begun pulling down the last of the desiccated autumn leaves.

Although it is possible to say that the rough lads in the streets are blind tools of the mosque and are excitable and irresponsible, the rejection of the Shah affects every level. Only fear of divided authority, lack of confidence in or ignorance of any alternative leaders, and fear for their own safety under a new order keep the Establishment loyal. Even strong and committed supporters give out contrary signals of which they themselves are scarcely aware: usually this is that 'he had made great mistakes, of course, great mistakes'. If you assent and suggest what they are, they will warm to it for a moment and congratulate you on having noticed too ... and then cautiously rein in and revert to the horrors of anarchy, the communists or the Russians.

But the point is being increasingly put. A prize example yesterday. I was told Senator Robert Byrd was here on a special mission from Carter. Correct. One man assured me he had come to give a private message to the Shah that he should leave as the use of military force was becoming indefensible. Another told me that he had come to give a message of support and that this had boosted the Shah's confidence and emboldened him to toughen his stand!

It is all like having a boil come to a head and about to burst:

one prick and the pressure will be relieved. Then there will be a mass hysterical outburst of joy and revolutionary ardour. Euphoria for a week or two when nothing else will be thought of – except the leaders of the two factions establishing their rival positions as quickly as they can. In the first instance the clergy will win, for I believe the situation is 10 to 1 in their favour.

I still think Iran as a nation can survive this convulsion and come through the other side. But it will be hard-line Leftish, puritanically Islamic, very nationalist – not pleasant, but still a country that can sort itself out over two to three years. And the people who made the Iran of the last fifteen years – who were created by it – are vanishing in front of one's eyes. The arch practitioners are in gaol, guilty by act of complicity; or have already fled. And the Westernised professionals are quitting and getting out. It no longer looks like their scene. None is coming forward and standing up for the king. They are destroying him – and thus no centre force or opinion can possibly emerge.

Big engineering contractors are in great difficulties over materials and manpower. Short-term expats are clamouring to leave – but there is no money to pay them, nor exit visas to give them. Typical tale of a big government agency, NIGC,[3] which lost every document and record they possessed in the arson on 5 November: three weeks later their managing director is ill in Europe and apprehensive at coming back because he is on the List. Meanwhile in the office the usual lack of a deputy and second-line management (his was an extreme case of a one-man band) are still looking shell-shocked and unable to throw up new leaders or decision makers. So all is deepening confusion.

Evening: I came back with not much to write about ... but then it broke. I sit at dinner, back by the skin of the curfew, with pictures of determined movements around Qolhak in my mind: troops moving nervously in the dark, bayonets and rifles at the ready, officers ahead with loudhailers, to take up positions – against their own people. And 'the people' – youths of 20 or so – furtively slipping by to goodness knows where. Something was on. Both sides were squaring up.

I got back and had sat down to dinner and was playing some music when Abdul[4] ran in to say that there was a great shouting in the distance. I went out into the cool garden (so mild for this time of year), scented with rain on dust. A great beat of sound in the distance came to my ears, mostly from the Qolhak direction, but even from the Pahlavi Avenue side too. I strained to hear. Tens of thousands of voices were shouting 'God is great' (*Allah-u Akbar*), ceaselessly punctuated by the rattle of gunfire and crackle of shots. On, on, unbroken, '*Allah-u Akbar, Allah* ...'. Dogs barked, like ourselves everyone was out in the garden listening, or telephoning frantically to friends. It sounded like the voice of doom.

Before the eruption, an intense word with Goudarzi. The violence came from 'them'. 'We' (the people) would only cry and shout. We took our guidance from the Agha (that same simple, homely respect for Khomeini). At the mention of the British and any suggestion that they (me, for that matter) were seen as the enemy, his eyes lit up and he said, 'The BBC was the speaker of truth – not falsehoods – but the truth.' We were loved for it as this was British, even though our government was with the Americans who were behind the Shah and were bad!

Where are they, those shouting crowds? Headed north, towards the Shah, lonely in the palace, awaiting his fate. The firing has died down. The troops overcome? Or, their hearts incapable of firing any more, they have thrown in their lot with the people? If so, then all is over and tonight is the end of it. It sounded as the Bastille must have done from afar.

Later: what had I been told? That the Tudeh were finally showing their hand. Released prisoners, Afghan labourers, the traditional old Tudeh cells, had all come out last night to provoke things. The result was a sharpening of the situation and the army/

government had had to change its attitude. There was to be a
coup with Azhari pushed aside to let the real hawks take over.
This would be Martial Law Commander Ovaissi, together with
Rabii⁵ of the air force, but the front man – and hardest of all –
would be Manouchehr Khosrowdad,⁶ the former Special Forces
commander and presently commander of the Army Air Wing
(helicopters) who was the Shah's last card and was totally, fiercely
loyal to him and to the monarchy (he is fast-living, a star show-
jumper, but a professional soldier and a martinet – and no doubt
quite ruthless). But if I were Hoveyda (reportedly moved to
harsher custody) or his poor colleagues, I would tremble at the
chant of the mob outside. They will demand immediate sacrifices.

SUNDAY, 3RD

People speak of last night as if it were a lark, a game. Much fun
at the use of loudhailers and tape-recorded demo noises to create
the illusion of multitudes. But there were two killed nevertheless.
Others speak of youths clad as martyrs in white sheets standing
on rooftops and crying *Allah-u Akbar* and being shot down. Others
cried to neighbours to come out onto the streets; and then
appealed to the troops not to shoot their brothers. Everywhere
was noise and an impression of unison. I will never forget that
distant clamour on the night air: it sounded like retribution finally
marching on the palace. The Apocalypse.

The curious cowboy air of events continues. During the day
there was sporadic shooting in town for no apparent reason. As I
was driving up in heavy traffic and milling pedestrians, a whiplash
of automatic fire was suddenly loosed off (into the air) about two
hundred yards away. People looked round curiously rather than
dashed for cover. Then the rooftops would fill up with people
craning to see where the action was coming from.

What is this – martial law, or not? What is this bravado about a hard-line military rule which would no longer handle the crowds of youths with the kid gloves that had been worn up to now (*sic*) but would liquidate those Tudeh, National Front and released prisoners who had dared to show their hand? But on what moral basis would they do it? For this is the problem for all of us: despite all the stability and progress the regime has brought, does it deserve to win when one looks at the corruption and double-dealing, at the foolish, bogus pretence and gestures of so much of it? Above all the monument to scandal and cynical exploitation of privilege as represented by Kish Island[7] – that apogee of corruption and near-sanctioned gangsterism (how I wish I nevertheless had seen it – the Last Days of Pompeii). That fellow Mahmoud 'Stanley' Monsef must be shown up as the most unscrupulous and scheming shark of all.

The real gloom of Moharram is descending. No spirits in any bars today for fifteen days. TV is just one long mournful wail and no pictures. What a down-casting, death-obsessed creed this Shi'a Islam is for all its pure abstract beauty. And so much of it concerned with agonising over the defeat of one faction in a political war 1,300 years ago! At least it's silent tonight – then unexpectedly the crack, and then another, and then a short burst of automatic fire only a few hundred yards away. Who is stalking whom? The lights snuff out at 10 p.m. Grope once again for the candles and the Camping Gaz burner.

The political situation seems inert – more and more polarised. There are the two sides in increasing confrontation, with the regime apparently (or so it is said) trying to build bridges. But either no one will serve, or there is no one of stature to serve. It is too far gone and no one is willing to risk his neck by association with the regime.

Clearly the Russians' line has hardened as they have seen that the present situation is at once insoluble and untenable. They must be looking very hard at the American (and Western) attitude, which seems so confused and uncertain. Carter unwittingly precipitated this, but now is unhappy at having to live with the consequences. His beautiful, liberal, human-righteous alternative is failing to appear – and his benevolent autocrat has had to become a harsh autocrat. Poor man, but I doubt if the Russians are showing much sympathy. Clearly if they feel the Americans could let the place slip, the temptation to meddle directly or, ultimately, to intervene will become increasingly strong. How else did they win Angola or Ethiopia (where they could afford to be breathtakingly bold) or more impudently – but totally successfully – Afghanistan?

So, in darker moments, one wonders if there is another side after all yet to show itself: whether we are witnessing the expiry of a class, the erosion of a Western position, and a fundamental reversal of historical geography. Of course the Russians, if they decide to take greater advantage of it, will do it by stealth and by hiding behind 'popular forces' whose voice can already be heard through the cries of 'God is Great'. Pah, where is the voice of Allah in Turkmenistan, in Kazakhstan?[8] One view here is that the Russians would fear unrest spreading into their own backyard from a resurgent Islam in Iran; but I really wonder if they lose much sleep over that, for they are always prepared to crush rather than conciliate.

So in such uncertain moments one is driven back to the right-wing position: there *is* no one but the Shah, and as he *won't* change, can't change, one has to live with him as he is. Sad that he isn't ideal, and has made grievous mistakes, but too bad – there is no one else to guarantee one's interests. A tenuous, dangerous, immoral argument (to any liberal) but one that has served for the support of every other right-wing dictator since the Second World War. Here, however, I must confess I feel it is too late, the prop is too vulnerable and has been too weakened by recent events to bear the weight. Which leaves only the army, with him or without him (if they do not hold together).

All rather gloomy and perhaps the consequence of reading too much of Kissinger in *Encounter* last night. But Kissinger is more than an academic after all.

MONDAY, 4TH

The situation is absolutely baffling, quite baffling. Is it all a game? Or is it serious? Are the clever Iranians fooling us all – and themselves besides, mark you? That one can even ask oneself such questions while people (kids mainly) are being killed each night, while buildings are being burned down dislocating the whole system, is remarkable.

Why even suggest it is a game? Because the Iranians have reduced that terrifying 'cry of the people' the other night to loud-hailers and crowd sounds on tape recorders; because the troops are largely loosing off into the air; because the kids (most of them in jeans and about 17 or 18) march around with impunity, insulting the Shah, praising Khomeini, smirking and laughing about it all with the soldiers. As one observer of a so-called fire-fight incident said, 'It looked more like a game of tag.'

At lunchtime I preferred to think that these isolated shots or rips of automatic fire were from a sinister new element: the Tudeh showing their hand and firing off shots to scare people, make them think that there was more opposition than there was. Yet it is all so casual. In two days we are already used in the office[9] to volleys going off around, below, above us and scarcely turning a hair, except to wander out onto the balcony and peer down to see where it might be coming from.

It could be a communist tactic. If so, why so tame? Why not shooting at people – or is that to come? Why not more bombs in restaurants? The Iranians are expert at assassination. Why no attempt on anyone? That is when one is induced to ask: is it all a game? But to do what? To justify a totally hard line? It seems so elaborate and ultimately a stupid way to go about things; but Iranians do think around corners. They cannot see straight or believe the problem is in themselves.

As bewilderment and bafflement grow, the voice of the BBC World Service (both the English and the Persian-language service) is becoming an obsession. With no rivals, with those studious tones (in English), or knowing voices (in Persian), it has become people's only link with the outside world, to many the real world. So they come to attribute to it power and design. It has totally revived the old Iranian conviction (not a myth, even the most educated will assert) of 'the hand of the English' (*dast-e Englis-ha*).

Of course, the thesis that it is all a game is not really tenable, even despite the irresponsible out-for-a-lark youths who seem to make up most of the bank-burning, slogan-shouting gangs. The organisation demands a degree of discipline and control that is demonstrably impossible for the Iranian character – even if paid to do it. They can fool even themselves with the confusion between fact and fiction – though hardly on such a mass scale. Could it then indeed be the Tudeh? One experienced foreign observer sensed a difference between the groups who cried at night and the tightly organised and trained groups who operated in daytime (today we had the first shots fired back, with an effective attack on the police station in Shah Reza Avenue from the flyover, which left one policeman dead).

So, whether a pretext is being contrived, or whether the Tudeh are emerging to take the initiative with violence, the day of the showdown draws near. Ardeshir Zahedi is said to be back in town and is no doubt in a huddle with Ovaissi and Khosrowdad. Is there going to be a real crackdown with mass shooting down of the gangs and a systematic selective elimination of Leftists, nationalists and ex-prisoners as there was in Indonesia and Chile? And then safety, so that we can all breathe freely? I sense it. A junta which will have to be rid of the Shah, execute Hoveyda & co. to show themselves even-handed ... and then savage the Left. One even hears talk of them 'razing Qom to the ground'.[10] God help us, the holocaust of mindless frenzy must then come about. The army would surely not do it. We are living in a crazy world just to talk of it. Much more important than razing Qom is to have their rank and file resist the call of Khomeini. If his appeal to the troops to desert falls on deaf ears, then he is finished. His last trick is trumped. We must wait and see.

As I write the BBC tells me that the French government has at last given Khomeini a sharp nudge. French soil is not to be used as 'a base for insurrection'. Quite right. Why does no one ever see a French hand behind all this?

TUESDAY, 5TH

Friends are leaving in droves. The comrades who remain feel at once lonely yet closer to one another. What do we fear? The worst is Northern Ireland or south Italian gun law with selective assassinations and indiscriminate bombings. That is why the naming of names in the Central Bank list caused so many shivers. What other lists are in preparation? Yet few who stay would not privately admit that the danger adds a certain spice, like mild rock-climbing. Still, there is a clear and early threshold whence it would cease to be 'an experience' or 'living through history'!

It is odd to think that Khomeini is a better-known face and character to a million television viewers in the UK than to ourselves. Is he a crazed old priest, or an implacable warrior of pure Islam? Is he independent, or is he served by and manipulated by – as his critics would say – communist sympathisers? But the force of his presence is shown by the way he came to dominate old Sanjabi when the latter went to see him in Paris. Certainly this projected Islamic world and society is one that even few Iranians know about. Who has ever heard that there is an English mullah in Shariatmadari's entourage in Qom? Few Iranians would credit it; but there is.[11]

What are the other clergy thinking? And what an embarrassing, even humiliating, mission it was for the Empress to go to Najaf to consult Ayatollah Kho'i[12] and try to persuade him to cleave to Shariatmadari and distance himself from Khomeini. Within an hour of hearing it, I had two estimates of Kho'i: he was senior even to Shariatmadari, let alone Khomeini, was the Pope of the Shi'as; alternatively, he was pro-Western – it was all a typical Pahlavi gimmick. Or even of King Hussein[13] going to see Khomeini, who, gossip has it, refused to receive him.

The situation could not be righted by a coup by some even harder-line military junta. They could no doubt liquidate the Tudeh and liberals and cow the mullahs for a short time – but they couldn't win the people round or the technocrats. They cannot even get a man of stature to head the great prize of NIOC.

There seems to be little doubt that the BBC Persian Service is biased and is subversive to morale, if not actually inflammatory. The public perceptions on this are too consistent to be ignored. I reckon that if a body broadcasts in a foreign language such as Persian to a volatile region, it has a grave responsibility to ensure that it does not open itself to the charge of partisanship and therefore of interference. People are quite obsessive on the BBC and it is colouring Iranian attitudes to Britain for years – far more effectively, for good or ill, than the embassy (and of course it could cut either way).

The next stage of personnel changes is under way: rumour of the recall of certain prestige ambassadors like Parviz Radji.[14] Soon one will have lost friends in most key places, and the slow revolution will have proceeded further.

WEDNESDAY, 6TH

These are critical hours. The enormity of what could be – the chaos, the ruin, the loss of the identity of Iran (though I think this would take some time) – is facing everyone. The fun, the good things, the spread of wealth (yes, everywhere) is remembered – the misjudgements, the trickery are being seen for the imposture they were. This is confession indeed. But must we, they, all be cast into hell fire? Why not? Other ruling classes – and that is what we are talking about – have been before. Look at the Romanovs, or the Bourbons. It can happen.

Still, tonight they are locked in debate: the politicians, the soldiers, the clergy, the soft-liners, the hard-liners. How to rid themselves of that turbulent priest? Does he stand for anything? Or is it really only what is alleged – a personal grudge (and that perhaps misplaced) between a priest and a king?

How can Islam be appeased? I had a fine if concentrated talk with a distinguished lawyer of one of the old families today. 'Pah!' he said. 'They [the mullahs] have nothing to teach us. They have said nothing new for 500 years, nay 1,300 years. I don't need to know them personally. They are all the same and always have been the same. The thing that concerns them most is in which hour, on which day, the moon passes from one month to another. Even now the concordat [the right term] that is being worked out with His Majesty [Ah, to hear that term again!] hinges on such mundane things: mixed schools [well, so what?], women in the army [nix], Western films and plays [so what?] and – the best – the fact that women policemen would be tolerated but should not wear trousers.'

I still don't believe the next few days are going to be a riot. I am still not frightened … if decidedly apprehensive. But 'the people' are against him (yes, they are – but do they really know why?).

Telephone news: Sanjabi released tonight. And the leading ayatollahs are to lead processions on the streets on Sunday. Irresistible
– like the Church in Poland. It just has to be lived with.

The town was calm, almost too calm, today. And silent tonight
– but at the moment of writing there is a spurt of nervous gunfire
nearby. And ... DAMN, the lights have just gone out.

THURSDAY, 7TH

A sudden start to apprehension. This is becoming serious. Feverish
attempts at composition are going on, but also moves to confront.
For the first time today my gardener was nervous. He tells me of
plans for a great march from Shah Abdol-Azim[15] towards Tehran
and ultimately to the Niavaran Palace. It will be led by the leading
ayatollahs, including Shariatmadari and – so his people are saying
– by the Agha (Khomeini) himself. The leaders will be dressed in
the white sheets of martyrs. What will the security force do?
'Shoot it down if we have to,' says one – 'that's what Reza Shah
did in the demonstrations against him.'

Can it be so terrible, so apocalyptic? There is still so much
good sense, so much common ground about. One thinks of a
Tehran traffic jam – everybody snarling, striking attitudes, being
selfish, even coming to blows. But then it frees itself and is soon
forgotten.

Who are behind the movement? It is not really the communists
or any outside power I am sure – it is religious fanaticism, religious
resentment, and envy and discontent in the lower middle classes.
It is destructive and hopelessly simple-minded: the Shah is all evil,
they say, and must go, and Khomeini is both leader and saviour.
Yet where is the very class that should be defending itself? Many
have already run and proved everything that was said about them
and in so doing undermined the moral basis of the present order
(hence the extraordinary impact of the List). Those that remain

have no institution through which to speak or write; and without
the press it is even more difficult to hear their voice. Someone
today said it was time for the great Iranian merchants and industrialists to come forward. They were trusted, had a following,
had shown they could achieve things – yet for the past four years
the very regime that had fostered them had kicked and hampered
them. Oh, sad terrible misjudgements springing from arrogance,
conceit and exaggerated ambitions. It springs from something deep
in the Iranian character. They cannot escape – most of them –
from themselves, yet hope for the saviour who is going to redeem
and transform them.

On Sunday and Monday if the army is asked to fire, it will
break up. Already the civilian labour in army camps has walked
out on strike. Goudarzi, who has a conscript son serving in Tehran,
says at least half the troops have turned away from the government. My friend has a simple-minded expectation, nay hope, that
the Agha himself will lead the marches on Sunday (can he walk?)
and then retire to meditate and pronounce from Qom or Mashad
where he would wish eventually to lay his bones. Goudarzi assures
me there is no threat to foreigners if we stay tight at home.
Regretfully, however, the advice of the local chapel, led by one
Agha Gowhari, is that though they would like to welcome me
among them at Ashura as last year, it is better for my safety that
I do not come this time. They look forward to seeing me next
year.

FRIDAY, 8TH

Everything so still and quiet. Indications that some compact has
been agreed between the clergy, the National Front and the
government on the processions. They will start from seven centres
and converge on Shahyad Square. If they are peaceful, there will
be no interference from the government. Every indication that

the Shah personally remains in charge – or at least that he is referred to. In an agony over the shootings of his own countrymen, he is said to have shifted with great reluctance from his instruction to shoot only in the air to an order to fire at their legs – but not to kill!

The herd continues to leave. The airport departure lounge is in pandemonium. One American journalist used the cliché of Dunkirk. He also indicated the degree of opportunity for the Russians if they ever decided to test Western resolve. He states flatly there was 'no way' that the US would intervene militarily after Vietnam. Yet I repeat: I don't despair. What we are witnessing – as we have from the outset – is traditional Islamic Iran taking advantage of the regime's weakness on economic and political grounds (Carter's admonitions) to claw back some of the ground it has lost in the last fifty years under the Pahlavis. It is not essentially Leftist; it is not foreign subversion; it is not foreign machinations: it is a domestic Iranian movement. And as the Shah's dream of a Westernised Iran was always problematical, and as he tripped himself up by his handling of the situation, the traditional forces so long on the defensive are now seizing their opportunity – and are probably surprising even themselves at the speed and extent of their success.

SATURDAY, 9TH

So we approach the brink. An extraordinary elation among friends today, a camaraderie, a devil-may-care spirit, intoxicatingly mixed with intense analysis and confession of personal reactions. An eve-of-Waterloo feeling. And it was foggy. A rare mild English fog descended by nightfall, still and pervasive. Yet tomorrow could be bright, clear and cold, such is the quicksilver weather in Iran at this time of year. They say 130,000 cars left the capital today. The streets are already half-deserted, every shop and office shuttered, barred and dark.

What scenes, on the one hand, of exhortation to the troops must be going on at this minute; and what solemn preparations of the *kafans* (white death shrouds) for the demonstrators who may well indeed be martyrs by this time tomorrow; and what alleged filling of thousands of bottles with benzene as Molotov cocktails. The danger now is anarchy. A massacre tomorrow, a mowing down of religious leaders and the faithful will lead to the most awful release of vengeance over the bodies of a shattered army – for I do not believe the army will hold fast. And that will be a wild, furious, anarchic vengeance which will be no respecter of persons or institutions as was the last rampage on 5 November. In a curious, mad kind of way, even that is now seen as largely stage-managed. Within set limits, obviously clearly understood (namely, no loss of life, only certain buildings, etcetera), anything went.

What are the Russians thinking in all this? No one asks them. I got furious with an American journalist last night who was talking on and on about two of the most famous men in town right now, Bill Sullivan (the US ambassador)[16] and Tony Parsons (his British counterpart). 'Why do you and all of your friends always keep consulting them?' I asked. 'Have none of you ever thought of calling on Vinogradov [the Russian ambassador]?' Silence: he hadn't. It had never occurred to him.

How we all confess to our own actions. Some are honest and say they sent their families away because they feared for their safety. Others aver, 'Well, it was nearly Christmas in any case so I thought she/they/we might go a little earlier.' Some even have the brass to say seriously that they went for Christmas shopping! And then the piecemeal stripping of households of their prize items. We have all done it and it is surprising how, with care, no one who hasn't known the house before can tell the difference! So much for our prized *objets d'art* and Persian carpets.

The teeming rain has stopped. The last car has screeched home.

It is still and silent and foggy. No *Allah-u Akbar*. No shots. We wait.

SUNDAY, 10TH (TASSU'A)[17]

Woken about 4.30 by the distant noise of heavy equipment moving and occasional dogs barking. The electricity didn't fail last night – there was too much for both sides to do. One pictures hundreds of thousands of mourners and determined young agitators preparing, many knowing that – God forbid, wanting that – they should die on the morrow. It is like the eve of a great set-piece battle. How can one be anything but apprehensive that this is too much to hold, too late, too much excitement, too much vengeance? And this is happening in every town in the land, not only in Tehran.

Later. It stayed mild, so it stayed foggy but not really wet. A great multitude *did* assemble; but the rules were observed. Whatever the BBC might have said – or hoped – it turned out to be a religious not a political occasion. The day seems to have been a triumph of trust and discipline. As Goudarzi said with shining eyes, 'I told you so. If they do not provoke us and shoot us, we are not men of killing and burning. Let us express ourselves as we want, and there cannot be any trouble.' I am told that it was Azhari, taking it on his personal responsibility as PM, who overrode the misgivings of Ovaissi and the others. God preserve him.

Out of all this, if there is to be any reconciliation, there have to be scapegoats, and clearly these must be Hoveyda and Nassiri at least. Hoveyda was not a bad man and I doubt if he feathered his own nest, but he was essentially frivolous and a showman, the impresario of the Great Iran Show. If there was any man whose conceit, arrogance and constant assurances that all was well was more culpable, it was ——[18] (but make no mistake – neither fooled the King).

What is the truth about the populist priest Khomeini? The view here is to see him as an embittered old cleric surrounded, mis-guided and goaded on by a coven of communists and Muslim radicals close to Qaddafi and the Palestinians (though neither are Shi'i) who wish to unseat or weaken the Shah as the great and good friend of the West, and of Israel in particular. And so to tip the balance one way just at the time when Camp David is tipping it in the other?[19] What a last laugh that would be!

MONDAY, 11TH (ASHURA)

Still, mild, grey and damp. All quiet. More great marches on Shahyad Square. Tried too late to get within distance of them but became embedded in a flood of cars and people. The town was effectively divided into two with troops and tanks making a cordon right across midtown from east to west. Easy to pass through to the south, but a great obstacle in getting back. Chastening to see – a temporary Maginot Line across a city shielding the homes of the rich, the foreigners (me included!), with the Shah and his palaces in the north. Yet once again all passed off peacefully. Now for the political changes to follow though I imagine the army will stay up front a week or two until clear dispositions have been made. But the people will expect a change sooner rather than later. After today, a picture of Khomeini hangs in Goudarzi's house.

This is going to be a pretty dismal, archaic puritanical Islam, with a strong anti-Western, if not pro-Eastern, bias. An Iran turned in on itself instead of the outward-looking Iran of the Shah's years. So many good flowers blighted. But then they never took root: they were artificial transplants, or kept in a greenhouse.

Iran is becoming foreign before one's eyes and reverting to itself.

TUESDAY, 12TH

Curfew back to 9 p.m. No reward for good behaviour. *Not* a sign of confidence.

Certainly a great change of mood today. Relief that the dreaded Ashura had passed off in almost festive spirit; but no relief that it had led to any solution. Rather a dread that the two sides have been exposed and that the situation can't hold like this while the country strangles itself. The rejection of the Shah seems even more complete. No one now gives him any real chance. At best it would be a phasing-out after some alternative order has been installed under him (Bazargan's view). His need to rely on open military power is so blatant that some think Carter may already be hinting at disengagement (having cracked the mirror in the first place, he now watches the glass disintegrating). Old hands comment on the State Department's undermining of their ambassador, Bill Sullivan – a sure sign of a change of policy. Also the thesis that the army itself may come to find the Shah a liability, and that they are already taking decisions without him, is gaining adherents.

Political initiatives seem to have come to nothing for the moment: the confrontation is too stark. If Ovaissi couldn't stomach Sharif-Emami's concessions to the press and parliament, how could they live with Amini or the National Front? Zahedi is posturing, hiding in a lot of hot air (or is this also a show?). Yet while there is relief that the old days are past, there seems to be a new kind of violence today. In the provinces more attacks on Savak offices that are still resisting. Outright battles then ensue. A dramatic report tonight of three soldiers armed with automatics opening fire on a room full of officers in the Imperial Guard barracks in Lavizan,[20] killing eight and wounding twenty-three; two of the three soldiers were killed in the return fire. This is the sort of story that is greedily heard, passed on – and therefore the stuff of psy-war.

Beyond all this – which few seem to see yet – are the nightmarish economic problems that lie ahead which could produce a revolution of desperation. Overcrowded cities that cannot be fed because there are no funds to pay for imported food; projects, factories, building sites that will never revive, with urban unemployment as a result; swollen government organisations that cannot occupy their half-trained staff. What a disaster. Who was to blame then for not seeing? Everyone now looks for a scapegoat – lack of 'intelligence' (but on what?), selfishness etcetera. Many, many knew the dangers, were aware of the discontent, yet were taken by surprise by the degree of organisation and violence, and the speed which was the consequence. It is astonishing to me that it hasn't happened sooner (how could the people stomach so much delusion and drivel?) ... but they did, and so one cravenly went along with it, and hoped one was being too pessimistic to think otherwise.

WEDNESDAY, 13TH

Today there is evidence of a counter-offensive ('counter-momentum' is the 'in' term) of rather more force than we have seen so far. New pro-Shah slogans are being sprayed or painted everywhere, crowds are coming out on to the streets in the provincial cities and shouting for the Shah, and fighting has broken out between rival groups. Above all has been the story of 'the dream' of another ayatollah, Qomi, one of the five most eminent religious leaders. It seems there had been a nasty dispute in the shrine at Mashad about the gold and silver cloth covering the tomb of Imam Reza which had been donated and placed there by the Shah.[21] Some wanted it now removed as a defilement. That night the ayatollah had a dream, a vision in which the Imam Reza himself appeared to him enquiring what all this trouble was about and asking why they were trying to destroy the only Shi'a king and the only Shi'a nation?

When Qomi recounted this the next day, news spread like wildfire and tens of thousands came out onto the streets, condemning Khomeini and praising the Shah. Khomeini, telephoned in Paris by Qomi, is said to have been taken ill as a result. Another delicious version has it that Qomi telephoned Khomeini to tell him personally. The latter, at a loss when faced with divine intervention, said that surely his colleague had been eating too much rice late at night! Thus chastened, Qomi retired the next night and was revisited by the Imam, accompanied by no less than his forebear Hazrat Ali himself, who ordered him to spread the word and who upbraided him for needing to consult others – and by telephone! A startled Qomi decided to tell all and wrote it down for the record.

Inspired? It must be – but surely not by the Imam Reza! Highly effective counter-propaganda. Weirder still and weirder. But facile and short-lived. Pure farce were things not so desperate.

I think all this is pushing things towards a stronger army hand. Azhari is sensible but out of his depth; Ovaissi sounds blunt and soldierly; Rabii and Habibollahi[22] hawkish. Yet without moving the Shah on, can they cope with the strikes? The strikers look implacable and there is no let-up from Khomeini who alone appears to command the movement. The economy and society cannot withstand this indefinitely.

Better reports of the Shah himself in private, but bewildered by the endless options and showing no signs of decision or leadership. He is not recovering his mastery of himself, let alone the situation. He intervenes haphazardly but is now not referred to on many executive matters. Surely the day must soon come when the officers find they can do without him and indeed that he is the obstacle to getting the people (intelligentsia and workers) to collaborate with them? Yet unless there is a coup of more radical, revolutionary officers, I cannot see the present generals ever trusting any combination of 'liberal' or clerical politicians.

Nor do they have – or have they ever have had – any contact with such politicians.

It is eerie to listen to the silence at five o'clock in the morning. The soft, mild fog persists. If it stays so mild it will not lift.

How badly the American name is suffering with the wholesale evacuation of US companies by special charter aircraft. It is leaving a profound feeling of lack of confidence and respect for them. It won't be forgotten. One vivid illustration: two bank offices in my building took down their plates as soon as their officers had left. Prudent? Sensible? Yes, but also somehow humiliating and guilty. I bet the Shah's picture has been taken off the wall and hidden in a drawer for future redeployment or destruction as appropriate. Rashly I still leave mine up.

THURSDAY, 14TH

In the aftermath, almost a silly season typified by 'the Dream'. Two Iranians have rung me to say 'It's all over now, then?' Many clearly believe in it! It is having a real effect. But I suspect the counter-move is thin and will soon peter out. The movement can command numbers and resources. Every monument and wall is now defaced: that scruffy infection in the university campus a few weeks ago has spread everywhere.

One has an odd feeling of living out a charade. Are passions really aroused? Or is it largely posturing and play-acting? From the revolution on tape recorders to 'the Dream', it seems spoof, fake. But then so much of Iran is, and so was much of the Shah/People Revolution, 2,500 years of monarchy, the Great Civilisation -- no one took it too seriously. Many laughed behind their hands. And why should Iran ever change? They cannot take themselves seriously. For most of them, appearance is all.

The only thing that has produced this trouble is economic discontent. The rest would have continued to be grumbled about but not fought over. And who are the main demonstrators? Less the industrial workers in the private sector (they struck first for money) than the government clerks, the bazaaris, the teachers, the students – those with some education and high expectations and many frustrations. The true intelligentsia wash their hands of it, or feel guilty, or both.

The National Front, for all the wish of some to be rid of the Shah, still automatically defers to him. Would he permit this? Would he support this? They have no self-confidence and no alternative plan of their own.

FRIDAY, 15TH

I stared it in the face today: took the dogs for a walk in superb sunshine to Darrakeh, one of the old villages of Shemiran.[23] Round the corner from the modern villas – suddenly one was in the Islamic Republic! Every black flag had its picture of bold-browed Khomeini, every wall was scrawled with the two incantations 'Praise to the Imam Khomeini' and 'Death to the Shah'. Everywhere, everywhere – overwhelming.

The mood has seized the people, become an obsession – and they have become different. Men proudly kept to themselves, unaccustomedly ill at ease even at greeting a foreigner; and I was followed by kids calling out 'Car-ter, Car-ter' or chanting 'Arya-mehr – Car-ter' (Shah – Carter).

The professionalism of the propaganda, like the organisation behind it, is astounding. Everywhere that frowning photograph; and a sort of silk-screen stencil which allows his features to be sprayed on the walls from aerosols; bulletins from the 'Islamic Movement' are posted on every shop with knots of people reading them; a group of students have Islamic (or Marxist?) pamphlets laid out on a table. I heard kids singing among themselves as they walked: 'Death to the Shah.' The hatred and the rejection are overpowering. Worst of all was the scene on a footpath leading to the mountain outside the village. A dead donkey lay sprawled across it, lying amid battered tins and its own dung. A skewer had been driven through its stomach. On it was one piece of paper which read: SHAH.

I came away fearful, chilled, for this is part of Tehran. Our wealthy streets and gardens are hostages embedded within this network of 'villages', each now a hotbed. One clings to the safety of the army and martial law – what happens when that goes, as it surely will? These people, like their religion, are intent on martyrdom and death.

With the vision of that totally disaffected village still in my mind, I reckon the laughing will soon have to stop – two to three weeks? One reason it must come soon is that all the people, even the revolutionaries, are getting fed up with the inconveniences of life. No cinema, interrupted TV, useless radio, no newspapers and – above all – no schools.

What is there to do? (Plenty actually! First day's skiing yesterday, a flawless day of marvellous pellucid Persian light.)

SATURDAY, 16TH

An ugly, irritable start. Streets jammed with traffic – but why, as there is no business? A wish that something decisive would happen one way or another, no matter what it would bring. Scenarios that a few weeks ago were spoken of with practicality and hope, now seem hollow and unreal. A free press! Elections! A coalition government! The Shah to be a constitutional monarch! The most ludicrous of all.

News of stick given by the army at Isfahan and Kashan, with helicopters flying in combat troops to beat the place up. Towns later barricaded off and traffic somehow diverted round them. How is one to escape from this growing confrontation of impassioned people and a strong, threatened, frustrated army? It could crumble amid terrible violence.

MONDAY, 18TH

I must put the vision of that rabid village out of my mind. If that was typical, then indeed we are lost. But was it?

I find that the fruits of that great, peaceful confrontation of Ashura are beginning to show. Each side saw the other's strength. The regime was on the defensive, but the army held (if not without some unnerving fraying at the edges). From that comes the present stand-off – with only the economy being ground to dust in between. Yet this itself is having an effect: people, merchants, bazaaris are getting fed up with the inconveniences, fed up with the loss of business. Weeks of it. Elections are over in a day, coups are over in a night – but this torment drags on. They have lived off their fat so far, but now it is beginning to waste the substance.

Khomeini is coming to seem more of a loner, a hopelessly stubborn old man, hardened in this by a personal score to settle, who is no more in touch with reality than the Shah is and who is surrounded with the same sort of court of sycophants (the breed can be revolutionaries too) telling him what they want him to hear or what he wants to hear. I am beginning to realise that the simple people do really think of Khomeini as a substitute for the Shah – and this is not just a talking point. Grotesque, but so far have things become oversimplified and unreal.

If the above faint hope is true, then perhaps serious talks can be undertaken with the National Front which could lead to a civilian government and the troops off the streets. I think the move has got to go as far across the political spectrum as the National Front to find people who can be trusted to work under the Shah without being seen as yet more 'bought' men. Once such a leadership emerges – and is believed in – then the many good men presently standing back could perhaps suddenly come forward to fill what appears to be an empty gulf between the crude army and the rampant, impassioned, dangerous Islamic movement. And behind all this are growing signs of the Left (I am told that Radio Moscow, and the Tudeh party radio from Leipzig – for long discounted as mere propaganda – will soon be rivalling the BBC in their audience).

One point on the simplistic idea of an Islamic republic: which Islam? The Kurds, the Baluchis, many Persian Gulf littoral people are Sunnis and would never accept a Shi'ite state. The Shah holds their loyalty because he has been seen – is seen – as above factional religion.

Lights out again tonight, dashing hopes that the previous nights' blessed uncut electricity might presage a return to good cheer in the house and a chance to read or write. What a roaring trade the opportunistic sellers of kerosene lamps from vans parked at street corners are doing! Mark-ups are two or three hundred per cent; 4 pence candles are selling for 20 pence apiece.

WEDNESDAY, 19TH

'He has a lock on the situation; he holds the dice.' Thus Khomeini is assessed by a foreign journalist, after three intensive weeks here. Many, many even of his own spiritual brethren, wish he would now go away so that they could enjoy the fruits of the ground they have won back; but he won't and is deep into the common people in a vivid, simplistic way. And he's no fool: he knows there is only one block to the Iran he wants and to his victory – only one. The rest would follow. One must admire his clear thinking. Meanwhile the National Front leaders seem a nice, well-meaning bunch but with no drive, no grip, no ideas on what to do. They are being carried along by the religious masses but can't set a direction of their own. Most are scared stiff of offending Khomeini; yet the most able people are still with the Shah. And Zahedi may yet be the political operator to keep one's eyes on. The old Tudeh party was another geriatric case and seemed to have neither organisation nor following. The rest of the Left were students with a Marxist fad and no serious following. They could make a noise and cause trouble but no more – though serious enough if the terrorist ever got his target: the Shah.

Despite reports of these classic army incidents we have all waited for – troops refusing to fire when appealed to by mullahs or demonstrators, and then summarily executed afterwards; or the Lavizan shooting affray led by a guards sergeant seeking to avenge the death of his brother in earlier riots – life is nevertheless seeping back. More shops are opening, even the bazaar itself today for two hours; banks are resuming, traffic is thick, smarter people are emerging from cover. Can it yet slowly be turned round? Or is this only a pause? The weather stays cool, still and fine, with the snow-covered mountains a standing temptation.

THURSDAY, 21ST

Fascinating talk to Parviz Tanavoli,[24] the most original yet the most 'Iranian' sculptor in Iran – someone who has established both a popular and an international name and who has been patronised by the Establishment yet never become part of it. He was confident, even excited that a fundamental change had already taken place – but had not yet been formalised – and that the true Iran was now about to show through. He was not worried by outside forces: the artificial era was past.

His sadness was for the Empress who had tried so hard and achieved so much, if in part carried away and misled by too many lobbyists exploiting her patronage. But in sum she had done more to revive traditional Iranian art and art forms than she had to introduce alien Western forms. Some of this work would be lost and the institutions (museums, galleries, etcetera) that had been established in recent years were too elaborate, too costly, too dependent on foreigners to find the going easy. Despite this, something new had been begun but had been inhibited by the repressive overall political and cultural climate. Tanavoli believed that the next ten years could be very exciting in Iran – a potentially true rather than a forced renaissance. He didn't fear the dead hand of Islam unduly. Iranian art had for centuries been infused with Islam – as his own was. He couldn't foresee a narrow puritanical Islam in Iran – it never had been like that: it would do no more than reject Western excesses.

But politically he thought the Shah had to go. If the Shah had had any chance of redemption left, he had forfeited it by his lack of public leadership in recent months. He was a block to new developments now. Sad, but a fact; and very sad for the Queen who had remained a simple and well-meaning person with something of the common touch that he, the Shah, so disastrously lacked.

SATURDAY, 23RD

It hit again today. There had been a blessed lull for several days with a drift back to some sort of work. Troops were only occasionally to be seen and the streets were choked again with traffic – usually hated but now seen as a sign of normality. Then came news of the assassination in Ahwaz: the acting head of OSCO (the Oil Services Company), George Link, had had his car bombed only a few weeks ago but had escaped. His successor, Peter Grimm, had had death threats but had carried on. Now automatic fire at a crossroads had got him. And two Iranian NIOC supervisors were killed in separate incidents.

What one most feared. The thing that will drive foreigners away more quickly than anything: efficient terror groups with specific targets. In the street, one had that ugly feeling one can get in Ireland of the enemy within. The dislike, the brutal hostility and the personal danger that the IRA has accustomed us to. How quickly it can sully and shadow one's view of people, that grip of personal fear.

Otherwise everyone seeking release in skiing. Vintage weather for days and, despite the snide BBC TV references to the 'elite' going skiing while the equivalent of Rome burned, ten thousand or more were up at Dizin today. So stories of the *pistes* and scarlet faces take some people's minds off the nasty feeling that nothing is solved and the ugly threat remains.

SUNDAY, 24TH (CHRISTMAS EVE)

Uptown, people resignedly speak of the Shah and the palace as 'holding on'. The Shah, Aslan Afshar[25] and a few other trusties remain. The family that insulated him has gone. The old counsellors have died off or are in gaol. He seems isolated and beleaguered, with the wrath and hatred of the people hardening against him more firmly and dangerously each day. Now the latest effort. A retired old Mussadeq politician, Dr Sadighi,[26] has failed as unacceptable to the present National Front leadership, to Qom and to Khomeini – and in the end to the Shah as well. The Shah has now no other option save the army (Azhari is said to have collapsed) and it is patently fraying at the edges.

It is the turnabout of the masses that everyone is astounded by, not least the educated Iranians. None thought they had been so out of touch with the ordinary people: but they had been. Those educated abroad feel a growing rejection, a sense of alienation in their own country. How much more the foreigners, even those of us who have travelled the country, who speak Persian and have a lot of Iranian friends – even we feel outsiders, exploiters, increasingly 'the enemy'. This is part of the trouble with the Shah himself who had drunk deeply of the West in his own few years at school in Switzerland so that it coloured all his attitudes and ambitions. He had contempt for traditional Islam – and showed it. Now he is being paid back.

And fear is growing: fear of the mob, fear of mindless revenge and envy, fear of retribution for the corruption. The people and the old forces are irresistibly taking over (dry rot it has been likened to) led by irresponsible, violent youth with nothing much to lose. And fear of a holocaust destroying a whole class if order broke down. This is what we try to put out of our minds.

Traditional Christmas carols at the embassy summer compound in Qolhak this evening round fiery charcoal braziers. But they couldn't be placed in front of the customary house as it was too near a neighbouring mosque and the Christian singing would be heard. Quite a lot of trouble downtown today now that the schools are back, with youths pelting stones at the US Embassy. I heard only the depressing beat of their chant and the accompanying rattle of helicopters, with kids prancing along Takht-e Jamshid Avenue[27] waving black flags.

It is said the Shah is almost detached about matters, playing it long in order to use every effort to produce a civilian government – in which he himself has scant belief – so that years hence when it has failed the people will turn again to him (his habitual identification with de Gaulle). Others say that senior officers are tiring of the Shah's restraints on hard action and are exasperated at his efforts to cobble together some futile cabinet of the centre while the security and economic situation deteriorates by the day. Patience is wearing thin.

Still brilliant and cold (it has been so for ten days or more) with a skin of ice on the pool. To Mass at the American Mission church. Ageless Father Williams,[28] twenty-two years ministering to his American and miscellaneous flock, has now become a coast-to-coast TV personality ('Venerable US pastor ministers to his flock though crisis rocks Iran' is the sort of headline). There they were, four hundred or so Americans, more men than women, with scores of Filipina girls (house servants and nannies mainly) among them. And the inevitable TV camera crew filming the scene to show 'how life carries on'.

MONDAY, 25TH (CHRISTMAS DAY)

Christmas lunch and flamenco guitar at the Spanish ambassador's (a friend of old)[29] with guests arriving late because of hostile demonstrations. As we celebrated, unmistakable sounds of heavy gunfire (tanks presumably) to the south.

My gardener later tells me four were killed at the Pich-e Shemiran crossroads, shaking his head in bewilderment. All so simple, he says: if only the Shah would accord respect to Khomeini and allow him back. Yes, respond I, but Khomeini says he won't return as long as the Shah is there. Are you surprised, retorts he, after he had driven him into exile for fifteen years and killed his father and his son?[30] Khomeini does not want to be, could not be, king. He only wants to die in his own Qom or Mashad and see his country live by a proper Islamic code. So, I ask, why is the Shah against him? Of course people have come to hate the Shah, he replies, whom they once obeyed and even loved. Why? Because he kills our boys (even though they seek martyrdom by provocation); because he holds on to mullahs and students as prisoners; because 'his people' have sent the wealth of the nation abroad (a reference to the List); and because he gives 'our' oil away to the foreigners. So the beginnings of anger arise even in my simple innocent Goudarzi.

Oh God, what a dismal religion this Shi'a Islam can be. All the streets hung with black flags, banners and drapes again today. All very well on a Christian Good Friday and one or two other days, but they wallow in it for weeks on end. Oh, for more sweetness, and warmth, and gentleness in their creed.

TUESDAY, 26TH (BOXING DAY)

Both good and bad in one. We gave our traditional 'open house'[31] and ate and drank, and sang carols, and danced the eightsome reel and had our hired *labou'i* (a street hawker) preparing steaming beetroots from his cart. But the day was dominated by guests' stories from downtown of the deteriorating situation, or by guests ringing up to say sorry but they couldn't face running the gauntlet of the rioters and the firing. So for all the Christmas spirit, worry and anxiety affected everyone. Every one of the Iranians – even of the old school – were quite open that the Shah was finished and that violence would only grow until he went; but that he would hang on unless pushed. Equally everyone was negative about any alternative, whether of an individual or an institution. After twenty-five years of political sterility, there *is* no one.

Most unnerving of all are the growing threats against in-dividuals. Someone very close to me today was threatened in a specific, vicious form which indicated he had been under close surveillance. Expats' domestic dogs have been poisoned. Mean-while oil production is down to derisory levels (500,000 barrels per day)[32] and coercion to overcome the strikes has failed. There are so many signs of an impending climax here. Delivery men are exacting tribute to supply basics – 3,000 rials tip today to deliver gasoil. Hoarding. People arming themselves in their homes. Only a matter of days, people now feel. Yet in the midst of it all, the power workers left the lights on over Christmas Eve.

WEDNESDAY, 27TH

A third day of roaming gangs of prancing kids and youths firing cars, obstructing streets with whatever they could find. All this with impunity, until suddenly there is a fusillade of shots and they are sent scurrying. Then a fair barrage of shots, automatic, and the crump of heavier guns. Nearly all the firing was into the air however, so the curious impression persists of the whole thing being a dangerous, slightly unserious lark.

Everyone feels things are building up to a climax – two or three days, many say. Partly it is the return of the kind of disorder mentioned above, but more the total failure of the authorities to overcome the strikes. The oilfields are virtually shut and only six days' petrol is left in the country. Central Bank is off again. Iranair is grounded. And the power workers switch on and off at will. Opinion against the Shah has widened and deepened. It has moved out from the masses to the middle and upper classes as they in turn have become convinced that no progress can be made, not even any return to normality, with him there. Yesterday I had one patrician of the old class tell me that even he thought the Shah had to go. Then one of H.I.M.'s personal cronies – a man who has benefited greatly from him – told me that in his view the Shah had to go and that he was only prolonging the violence by hanging on.

With this upsurge of opinion repressed for so long, one senses the true mass movement of a revolution that carries everything along with it and is so powerful that it changes the course of its own riverbed. All could be gone, swept away or picked off – oneself too, and one has to adjust to the idea without getting too depressed or even panicky. Looking around those sullen faces in the street, who is friend, who enemy, watching you, waiting for his chance, storing it all up for later use? Are there some young thugs cruising around in their battered Peykan cars, or some more calculating radical students who have one's name on some list already?

Political prognostications: that Sadighi is a dead (or lame) duck even before he has begun – nor can he begin without support from the National Front or the clergy; that a military coup by the hard-liners is in the offing; that the military must be coming to see the Shah as a liability; but that these *timsars* (generals) are too closely associated with him, and that some colonels or majors must make a real coup and throw in their lot with the Islamic nationalist forces and then lead them. In short, is a new Reza Khan[33] awaiting his moment in some barracks somewhere? A conservative Muslim nationalist officer though, not a Westernising nationalist such as Reza Shah proved to be.

THURSDAY, 28TH

I am in the petrol queue, for three hours. The ritual violence begins about 8.30. A pyre of black smoke went up near Qolhak. Then the snap and rattle of fire and crump of armour. Cars immediately start behaving nervously and horns sound like frightened cattle. People in the kerosene queue – young and old, women in *chadors*, young toughs – become agitated. When is this going to come to a head? Neither side is getting anywhere by this hit-and-run violence. Khomeini has seized them by his boldness, his steadfastness, his consistency, his simplicity. This is what political leadership is about: not whether he is less or more *daneshmand* (learned) than old Shariatmadari.

The crunch is on – no doubt. Oil production down to a trickle with the prospect of a total loss of petrol in a matter of days: kerosene queues of the miserable, two hundred yards long; Central Bank out; commercial banks out; all international telephone and telex out; and tonight a blackout of unprecedented length from 5.15 until now (9.45). As I write, the shouting starts again. A cold grey night, with chants in the distance: but no shots, not one.

The friends of the West are losing heart. More and more they are giving up and saying it is all the communists, with religion only as a front; that the Americans and particularly the British have let them down in the last year (how?). They are vitriolic about the provocation and distortion of the BBC.

I gather that the impresario behind Dr Sadighi is Ali Amini –

and that the former is likely to take office on Sunday next ... with presumably the true army coup to follow when he fails.

FRIDAY, 29TH

Excitement today (gloriously fine and mild again) with talk of a serious combination: Shapour Bakhtiar of the National Front,[34] proposed by Ardeshir Zahedi of all people! Could unite the main body of the National Front, the moderate clergy and the hard-line army men. The price? The departure of the Shah on prolonged vacation, but retaining titular powers.

Also a warning by Carter of precautionary movement of the Seventh Fleet to the Persian Gulf to deter any mischief by the Soviet Union – which at last seems to be stirring. The crunch is getting crunchier.

SATURDAY, 30TH

Growing drama and growing anxiety. Unable to assess the scores of warnings about trouble in town, we decided to go skiing and risk alleged stone-throwing villagers. Superb, on a day of flawless clarity, fresh powder snow and a sky of the deepest blue. No slogans scrawled up there but one felt the villages one passed through sullen and uncomfortable. A Iranian woman skier re-marked tartly in the queue that she saw there were still some foreigners left around (bitch!).

Then back to the now ritual social telephoning, discussion, worrying, trying to put a brave face on it. But things have worsened. We had to drive past rubbish fires in the streets, youths gathered in sullen knots around them. A march was coming down from Tajrish. Reports of much firing, deaths, a shuttered town; and from the provinces of attacks on British Council premises and the US and Turkish consulates.

Depression and perplexity over Bakhtiar, now repudiated and expelled by his own National Front colleagues. What made him go out on such a limb? It could only have been the promise of the Shah's departure. He must be getting ready to go. The aged Queen Mum, his mother, has left. She must have been in one of those two helicopters that clattered overhead at 5 p.m. last night in the evening sun. As there were two, it could have been H.I.M. himself, so I waved a farewell salute just in case. Perhaps now he will leave tomorrow with a new government installed.

Some say it is all a clever ruse to split the National Front, demonstrate that no civilian government is possible, and so give a pretext for harsh military rule by Generals Ovaissi, Gharabaghi, Rabii, Khosrowdad, Habibollahi ... and Azhari. If so, total disaster and revolution. I must still believe that Shapour Bakhtiar knows what he is doing. Meanwhile we calmly but seriously continue our conversations by candlelight before the log fire on how we will deal with our two dogs (put them down or leave them in the care of old Goudarzi – and hope we can retrieve them later?); where we could conceivably store our remaining personal things and hope to see them again; and how we would get our two Bangladeshi domestics safely out and back to Dacca. One now has to think hard and practically of such things instead of just worrying about them.

The cold, still silence of the curfew night, with abandoned, hungry dogs beginning to curdle the blood slightly with their howls and whines.

SUNDAY, 31ST

The day is dominated by the embassy advice (not instructions) to leave. Worried consultations with friends. Some stout and robust; others nervy; everyone concerned. The town itself is quieter though. To cap all, the rubbish men have gone on strike and youths set fire to the garbage heaps scattered in the streets. Troops blocked certain streets and some gangs went around shouting. What a soiled, graffiti-scrawled mess the town is becoming. Increasingly empty too as the petrol strike bites.

Then off in evening dress (concealed under top coats) to some German friends to see in the New Year.

JANUARY 1979

'The Shah Has Gone'

January 1979 was to be the final month of the Pahlavis. Nerves were more on edge. There was increasing talk of a coup by hard-line army officers, encouraged by Zahedi, himself supported by a hard-line group in Washington headed by the National Security Adviser, Zbigniew Brzezinski, who bafflingly seemed to be taking a different line from the Secretary of State, Cyrus Vance – though both were serving under Carter. A mysterious emissary arrived, General Robert Huyser, Deputy US Commander in Europe, allegedly to restrain the military hotheads and to assess the situation independently of Ambassador Sullivan. Meanwhile in the streets and even the countryside a more hostile attitude to foreigners became apparent.

Rising above it all was the growing presence of that implacable priest the Ayatollah Ruhollah Moussavi Khomeini, delivering his pronouncements from his villa in a Paris suburb. Khomeini was now almost besieged by the world's press and television, and he and his propaganda impact in Iran were inevitably given a tremendous boost. Counterpoint to this was the growing talk of the Shah's departure – no longer if, but when. Meanwhile Bakhtiar accepted the poisoned chalice of the premiership from the Shah on 6 January and formed a cabinet of mainly 'clean' technocrats. Only a few days later Khomeini, from Paris, established a Provisional Islamic Revolutionary Council, in which came the first mention of names that were to dominate the next stage of the drama.

On 16 January at 12.15 p.m. the Shah left – this event was followed by an outburst of spontaneous exultation on the part of the masses.

Bakhtiar's position looked increasingly untenable. The movement began to organise itself openly on the ground through local committees (the soon-to-be-notorious komitehs*) and retail co-operatives. Meanwhile amid growing turmoil on the streets, some of the worst shooting affrays of the whole rebellion took place in Tehran and provincial towns. Various emissaries visited Khomeini in Neauphle-le-Château, but none succeeded in persuading him to compromise with the 'illegal usurper and foreign puppet', the term he used for Bakhtiar's government, or in deflecting him from his fixed purpose of establishing an Islamic government.*

With the Shah gone, the round of rumours concerned when and how Khomeini would return. Three times it was to be on, only to be put off; but at last Bakhtiar conceded that the airport should be opened for three days to allow the great man to return. The strike was then lifted. In that window of opportunity I took my leave on 31 January.

Khomeini returned in overwhelming triumph the following day, 1 February. The Pahlavi regime finally collapsed on the 11th.

MONDAY, 1ST

Snug in our lair, nine of us drank, ate and sang it in with 'Auld Lang Syne'. And played charades until 4 a.m.! Reality again in the morning, so fine and mild one expects to see the buds bursting.

Bakhtiar is said to have wider support within the National Front; that Sanjabi is a dangerously silly old goat, overawed and intimidated by Khomeini. But that Bazargan is with Bakhtiar, it is said, and through him, the Qom ayatollahs. More and more openly there is talk that the Shah is about to leave for medical treatment abroad. No one is jumping up and down yet, but relief among senior Iranians and expats is widespread. Against this tenuous hope is the sombre news of the clashes and bloodshed in Mashad.

The most disagreeable thing is this welling up of popular resentment and hostility against the well-to-do and foreigners. One comes to feel guilty about things one had taken as a matter of course – skiing, a big car, a driver and household staff. It is hard to picture oneself as the 'elite' and privileged – until the masses point it out to one! People have been jostled or attacked simply for being in a Range Rover or even a BMW, both unremarked on until a few weeks ago. Yet everyone has noticed that the power workers did not cut off the electricity on Christmas Eve, and again on New Year's Eve. No accident. So there is some mercy and friendship somewhere.

Reports that the town is even quieter today – largely deserted as everyone stays at home to conserve gasoline. But also reports that Khomeini's instructions to the striking oil workers to produce enough oil for domestic purposes (thanks be to Allah, the winter has been extraordinarily mild so far) will be heeded and that Ayatollah Taleghani[1] issued instructions to this effect to Chairman Entezam in the NIOC offices. What an extraordinary demonstration of where the power really lies! Yet if the New Year's Eve power supply was one thing, it cannot be coincidental that the ground and air controllers have struck at Mehrabad airport, thus neatly and effectively blocking off the flight of foreigners following the advice of their various embassies to leave.

Assassination must be in the air. Shapour Bakhtiar is an obvious candidate. But could someone turn on the Shah to make a clear-cut result and prevent him slipping away unscathed? Later, gleams of hope about Bakhtiar from friends. The sort of people, indeed the people I would like to see rallying and committing themselves, are stirring. Substantial National Front men, said to be among the liberal technocrats, some of the honest ones who had been put, or put themselves aside, are associating with Bakhtiar such as Bazargan, Hassibi, Zirakzadeh – though vacillating. Talk of General Djam returning. And of Amini and Sadighi active in support.

Town quieter. Odd firing. Interminable lines of cars by the one or two petrol stations which have some hope of supplies. Hardly any office answers the telephone. Horrifying tales of the clash in Mashad – sounds as if the troops were overcome. Accounts of soldiers being lynched from trees and having their noses cut off. A fair amount of harassment of foreigners in recent days. If a car gets caught in a mob, it is badly beaten up and the driver is hauled out and roughed up. Best thing is to display a Khomeini sticker or, better still, to have one of his tapes running on the car stereo.

All is going on behind the scenes. Frantic pressurising of people who might be tempted to work with Bakhtiar. Telephone calls at all hours. His own colleagues are trying to isolate him, as much out of jealousy as disagreement. Yet he made a good impression on the radio. It seems the army is having cold feet on letting the king go – and they told him so on Friday. So the 'medical treatment' pretext is being denied. Meanwhile in the oilfields, Bazargan himself was booed: we have the power and we'll call the tune, the workers said. Even Khomeini's writ does not run there, it seems, so far have things got out of hand.

Derring-do of a British friend[2] who drove with his wife 1,400 km in a vanette from Bandar Abbas during the petrol strike. The question everywhere: are you American? When not, only helpfulness. Devotion to the BBC everywhere – 100 per cent audience. Every town, every village was saturated with Khomeini. Not a statue of the Shah was standing or, if too big to topple, not daubed or defaced. Qom was a dead town with urchins burning tyres and rubbish in the streets. The street bonfires that have become a feature of recent nights were first encountered on the outskirts of Tehran, supervised by older men while colleagues directed the traffic round them. The Shah's decline is irreversible was his conclusion.

In each workshop, men are divided between willingness to give Bakhtiar a try, and those who want no half-measures when victory is so near. Meanwhile behind all this lies the army, making increasingly wild and hawkish sounds – Ovaissi, Khosrowdad, Rabii.

God help us. It will be appalling if they step in and seek to shoot this down. Madness.

Should one think of working with him? Think what I have said so often about Kenyatta and the need to work with the man who can command, and therefore calm, the people – and Kenyatta seemed even worse than Khomeini in his time.[3] Is Sanjabi therefore right that Bakhtiar is putting the victory at risk just as it is about to be won?

WEDNESDAY, 3RD

The town largely deserted. A handful of cars. Where are they? In amazing queues, some a mile long at least, winding around blocks, down highways, and eventually reaching some besieged gas station, itself invested with jumpy troops and milling drivers. More pathetic are the queues of poorer people waiting for kerosene for their stoves. Thank God the spectacularly fine weather continues. I have never known it milder or the sky more brilliant. People can at least enjoy that in the queues.

All this is against the background of sombre news of increasing violence and atrocities. The usual pattern – Mashad, Kermanshah, Isfahan and now Qazvin – is of provocation to soldiers, even deliberate knifing and murder (Mashad, they say, began over an officer visiting his wife in hospital where he was savaged); officers finally lose patience and fire into the crowds; the crowds then go wild; general bloodshed ensues. Then it is all the fault of the tyrannous troops – a deliberate tactic to stir up the people. This swelling tide of fanaticism and latent hysteria in people: one can see them change in front of one's eyes. Usually the streets are now full of women in full black veils (*chadors*), often betraying that they scarcely know how to wear them. People seem to reck little for their comfort or even livelihood. It is a dark passion, a zeal, a commitment that has seized them.

The spiritual power of this man Khomeini is something I have never witnessed or even imagined. He is a great medieval force, a great leader of the regeneration of Islam – and not only in Iran. I learned today that he wrote his treatise 'Islamic Government: the Guardianship of the Clergy' in 1971 when in exile in Najaf and that this is now the lodestar for many. A return to fundamental Islam where church and state are one – and therefore no need of a parliament. Each ministry to have its own religious council, etcetera, etcetera. The most impressive thing of all is the degree of organisation of the Islamic movement, its all-pervasiveness and consistency. Its professionalism in propaganda by word, bulletins and 'happenings' is right up to date in impact and conception. It must operate its distribution system of tapes, *e'elamieh* (announcements), and stencils through an alternative society rather than an underground.

Hopes are now pinned on Bakhtiar who was confirmed as PM by the Majles today. Yet everyone fears his early assassination if successful. It is now war to the knife. The tragedy is that that silly old ninny of a Sanjabi has clearly become spellbound by Khomeini. Without having seen or even heard him on radio or the box, one can feel the drama and force of the Ayatollah's personality from those beetle brows and jutting chin (a facetious observation of mine: take his turban and beard away and he would seem to have a passing resemblance to Reza Shah – his sternness, those eyes!).

More tales of my friend's trip by car from Bandar Abbas. In the silent, sinister streets of Qom was something even worse than my dead donkey: a phallus-like pillar in the middle of a street surmounted by a dead dog and a dead cat. 'The Shah', read the placard on it.

The day ends on a hopeful note. Bakhtiar has a press conference where he not only says but does sensible things: no oil to Israel or South Africa; the Shah to go on leave when all in order and to be welcome to return; Khomeini free to come back; and the press to restart. One has to restrain one's hope for the end of the immediate strangling crisis and excitement at the prospect of sensible government without the excesses and false theatricals of the past.

THURSDAY, 4TH

A day of contrasts. A morning of growing hope and cheer for Bakhtiar. For myself, of commitment, of being on the fringes of cabinet-making through friends, of encouraging waverers. But during the day the excitement wore off and that leaden feeling of near-hopelessness seeped in again. One is not being naïve to think of Bakhtiar: it is the last hope of anything reasonable and constitutional. Just to say that, however, is to reveal its fragility. On one side the main plank of the deal is being withdrawn: the Shah's departure under pressure from the army. On the other, Shapour is already being branded as a collaborator, and the fury and venom is being turned on him and those who have dared to associate themselves with him. The sound, the feeling, of the real irresistible opposition is unchanged.

By night (after a last 'wartime' party round a log fire eating French cheeses) the dread returned. The shouting began again, as loud as it had been that first occasion – 'Death to the Shah'. Fear of the mob, of isolation, of being too late and trapped, returned. That gnawing indecision between one's wish to stay and not get rattled, and the urge to run and be out of it. But a log fire is a comfort, and after all it will be daylight again tomorrow!

One fears that Bakhtiar and his men (several one's friends – for some of whom one trembles at their inexperience and optimism) are going to be decimated. Then one looks for hope and remembers even this morning when the pall half lifted and one began to think that normal life and normal pleasure might return. Where one could live and plan (very important) again, instead of just hunkering down and fighting off anxiety and apprehension.

For the record, some of the names that were spoken of today: Bakhtiar for PM and War, Bani-Ahmad (Agriculture), Lahiji (Justice), Hassibi (PTT), Bazargan (Information), Madani (Interior), Darakhshesh (Education), Haj Seyed-Javadi (Higher Education), Adamiat (Transport), Pirasteh (Finance),[4] Minachi (Economy), Chief of Staff (Djam or Gharabaghi), Behazin (spokesman). The Regency Council: Shariatmadari, Djam, Bakhtiar, Sa'id, Sajjadi.[5]

All could come right so soon – but the Priest won't take the lock off. Implacable. He is utterly single-minded. A great man of his kind, give him his due. And tonight he asks why the Shah should be encouraged to leave – 'rather he should be brought to justice and tried by Islamic law'. Shudders (as those already in detention must be shuddering). As the shouting and sporadic firing died down we heard that Ovaissi had left the country in disgust at the Shah's handling of the situation and at the Bakhtiar government. Now what will the army do? Is the Ayatollah's moment at hand? He and only he is driving them on to its total, conclusive, violent, apocalyptic end. The rest would settle for a muddle if they could. He is clearly a Great Man, with a great and highly expert propaganda and psychological warfare machine. Unbeatable, I judge.

FRIDAY, 5TH

Everyone is waiting – apart from those feverishly trying to put it together and apply pressure. I sense an awareness that there is only one great decision left and that it must be imminent. The departure of Ovaissi is seen as a sign that Bakhtiar has more clout than was thought, that his base lies in an alliance with the moderate generals. My touchstone, old Goudarzi, tells me the army is divided with many, many of them National Front by inclination. But some remain loyal to the Shah. Fifty fifty, he says, quoting his conscript son.

Sunday sounds a day of menace – but from whom? The
National Front – when half of them are in the government (or say
they will be)? I will always remember Rustam Pirasteh's bemused,
bewildered mood the evening before he took office.

SATURDAY, 6TH

At last, a day of events and not speculation. First heard the Bakhtiar list on the radio at midday. Not the strength expected, except
for Djam, Mirfendereski (anything to get his own back?)[6] and
Pirasteh. The rest are unknowns, apart from his own cousin Abbas-
Qoli Bakhtiar. In short, the National Front have turned their backs
on him. The weather continues soft, warm and bright. Quite
unreal. The people see it as a sign of the Lord's support.

Then shortly after 2 p.m. a friend, an industrialist, rings excitedly
to say that he has heard the Shah in his own voice on the wireless:
that he is going – on vacation of course. He will return to reign
under the constitution; and Bakhtiar says he hopes to see him
return. It sinks in: the deal was there all the time – and Djam saw
to the ousting of Ovaissi and the hawks.

By 5 p.m. the newspapers were back. Jubilation in town with
cars honking and flashing their lights, and excited queues forming
to buy the papers, even longer than the usual queues for petrol
(from which much discipline has been learned). And what faces us
from the front page? The august, stern, humble, meditative, commanding presence of Khomeini. Goudarzi had tears in his eyes as
he brought me my copy. 'This is He for whom so many have been
killed,' he said. The degree to which this priest has gripped the
hearts of the people is astonishing. He looks invincible, I have to
admit.

Now the doubts flood in. Bakhtiar looks more and more to be
only a transitional figure, an opener of the way, provided he is not
treated harshly as some quisling who admitted the Shah's legiti-

macy by accepting office from him and, in so doing, acted to preserve the throne. He is of course playing the army carefully and carrying them with him so far – he can turn more radical once the deed is done.

Extraordinary to watch television tonight (in so far as one was able to through a broadcast fractured by power cuts). There they were, the new ministers, standing in that habitually submissive file before the Shah who appeared to be his usual upright, soft-spoken, modest but aloof self. The handshake, the inclination of the head, the look of awe. The aura clearly remains! Will they too fall for it even at this juncture? This is why critics of the regime distrust Bakhtiar's tactics and fear he has compromised himself, for all his good intentions. As one feared and expected, Khomeini has given an emphatic thumbs-down to Bakhtiar. So on to the revolution it is. He has the legions. Bakhtiar has made the breach, but the imperial castle has not yet fallen even though the commander has lost control of events.

The weather turns grey and colder. No apparent relief to any strikes except that the papers are back – *Ettela'at* showing itself more radical than *Kayhan*. The Inter-Con hotel is a hive of journalists.[7] A mixture of cowboy and high IQ. Sweaters, jeans, open-neck shirts and beards are the rule (with certain correspondents studiously different in well-cut suits and striped shirts). Camera teams and TV technicians wander in and out. Over sixty there alone. The greatest concentration since Vietnam, they say, and most of the Saigon brigade are among them. No one else in the hotel except for ambassadors having lunch – hosted by note-taking journalists! A cheerful bunch. It turned much colder tonight.

The oddest things can happen. Today I rang one of the (erstwhile) richest industrialists in Iran. 'Is he in?' 'No, he's in prison,' was the answer. (I knew he wasn't.) 'Why?' I enquired. 'Because he sent 150 million dollars out of the country.' 'Who are you?' I asked. 'One of his servants,' he replied.

MONDAY, 8TH

Another day of the Priest and the King. The latter defeated, bitter and reluctant; the other majestic, unbending and terrifying. This is going to be seen through to the end, and poor, honest Bakhtiar is the earnest, well-meaning piggy-in-the-middle. In the morning I was buoyed up by the comments of ordinary people. They had taken to Bakhtiar: they thought he was speaking the truth, was honest. In short, a good man. More and more it comes out that what people have hated, really hated, has been twenty years of lies and propaganda and flattery stuffed down their throats (hadn't one often felt the same?). They sense a breath of fresh clean air (from the newspapers, even from television) and exult in it.

In town it was a confused day. Parts entirely quiet, others the scene of more determined marches of older men (30 to 40 years old) with a more disciplined shout of 'Death to the Shah'. People who know no Persian can almost parrot by now the cry of *Marg bar Shah*, and even its scrawled script in graffiti is becoming recognisable to them. In one demo a crowd was suddenly confronted by armed soldiers coming up from Shah Reza Avenue. The crowd yelled, 'Soldiers, Brothers.' The troops relaxed, began to smile, lowered their automatics, laughed ... then mingled with the crowd. Thus it is falling apart. Elsewhere it is a very different story. In Mashad it all began with an attack on officers, and in Qazvin too,[8] with the result that the army lost its temper and drove tanks into the crowds or (as in Qazvin) simply terrorised the town. Officers are confused and uncertain what to do.

Tonight a rumour that Djam had turned his commission down and returned to London – which would be a hard blow for Bakhtiar. But is it true? And who is to succeed Ovaissi as Ground Forces Commander? An army and an opposition approach one another head on. Certainly there seems no move towards Bakhtiar from the religious. He seems to be both Persian and European in his political approach: Persian in that he is trying to humour the Shah to leave, while trying to save his face; European in doing the thing reasonably, legally. But we are in a situation of violence, retribution and hatred. Why, I ask myself – for all the liking and respect I have had for him – should the Shah escape when poor Hoveyda is to be tried and no doubt hanged, and Nassiri and Nikpay too (bravely trying to look assured and cheerful in their photos, but wasted and strained)? Meanwhile Khomeini, the implacable, the invincible, the intransigent, sounds sombre warnings. He scents total victory and running Bakhtiar off the scene.

TUESDAY, 9TH

Now the misery sets in. Winter has at last come. Scenes of a cold hell round the filling stations as people mill around in the snow and slush in the dark, shouted at by soldiers trying to keep control and firing occasional warning shots in the air. The government is not getting a grip and there is utter despondency in town. Ministers are not working. More and more there is talk of revolution, not reform.

Yet there were more cars back and a semblance of activity. No one obeys traffic signals or one-way streets. It is just every man for himself. What seems to be organised – and that on a grand scale – is disruption, demonstration and destruction. Yet something to remark on is that organisations that before were heavily dependent on expatriates continue to run after a fashion.

And what of the expats? We, the British community, are now down from around some 14,000 to 1,800 in Tehran, with 1,200 or so still scattered in the provinces – perhaps 3,000 in all. More and more we get to know one another. Small groups with great camaraderie. Get-togethers are arranged at short notice, like the convivial gathering at a friend's house in the snow tonight. Then off on our separate ways to our homes to huddle in front of the log fire (presuming there is no butane left, and only enough fuel oil to keep the water hot) and our candles and Camping Gaz lamps (for those who still have any canisters left). Even for those who laid in great stocks of everything, the end is in sight as the crisis persists and deepens.

I cannot see a military coup. Those who know the army cannot see that there are senior officers capable of commanding or organising it. Nor would the army follow. That brilliant opposition, informed with all the latest psy-war techniques, knows it. It sets out at one and the same time to provoke the army into atrocities, and to seduce it with brotherliness.

WEDNESDAY, IOTH

The winter has come and the screw is ever more tightly on. Three power cuts today. No relenting. Mist, snow and slush. First signs of desperation: people are tearing down dead branches from trees and burning them in the streets beside the *naft* (kerosene) queues – where the most wretched wait resignedly in file – or the petrol lines. People are leaving their cars unattended overnight, for two or even more days, and no one is interfering with them. A fiery youth to whom I gave a lift this morning told me how 'the people' had dealt with some army officers who had taken advantage of their curfew vigil to store up some jerry cans of petrol which they were now selling at 100 rials a litre. The papers are full of Sanjabi's press conference, more or less pleading for a position in Khomeini's 'government'. It looks quite irresistible.

I drove down to the ministry areas (more trees being dismembered or burnt) through half-deserted streets. No guard even on the gate. I went into a building normally hectic with comings and goings, the Finance Ministry. No electricity, no lifts, so I walked up to the eighth floor. Not even any lights on. I wandered around the deserted offices of vice-ministers and there was no one to stop me.

There hardly is a government: nine ministers were prevented by their staffs from taking possession of their own offices – just as the Agha had commanded. What magisterial authority, what effect! Lunch with an old-school Anglophile, touchingly but alarmingly sincere. In fairness he had been a critic for years, had known the feeling of the people and had long forecast doom. Now it was here. All the fault of the shallow Americans – we British were somehow excused as being much more subtle. In any case the voice of the BBC had saved us. It represented truth and the people truly were thankful to us for it. He was not appalled by the thought of Khomeini. The Ayatollah was a true Muslim and would restore Iran to its true and rightful character. He recked nothing for the communists – the Tudeh were played out – while the Marxists, the *feda'yian,* were active but could never command the people's support.

My lunch companion gave an account of Sadighi's abortive attempts to form a government that threw much light on the Shah's attitude of mind. Alone with the Shah, Sadighi said he had been unable to get people to serve under him. 'Why?' the Shah asked. Embarrassed, Sadighi said it was because they would not associate themselves with him, the Shah. At this the Shah snapped, leant forward, thrust out his arms and almost shouted, 'Why, why? I do not understand.'

In the morning I had visited Tavanir, the central power generating company, a client of the bank. There a washed-out, exhausted managing director had told me there were three kinds of power cuts: the daytime ones which were increasingly due to the inability of the power stations to cope with the load due to fuel shortages; second what we had today, the technical breakdown of the system due to snow and ice; and then the political ones that we had in the evenings immediately after the BBC Persian Service bulletin!

Talk, talk, talk of a military coup. By who? Khosrowdad? Rabii?

And who would follow them? And what would they do – a thorough military operation to invest cities, take out the ringleaders at night and shoot them? Quite unreal even to think of it. More think a coup might be the last act of desperation in order to try to save their own skins – at least the High Command. The vicious attacks on officers and NCOs in Mashad, Qazvin and elsewhere point the lesson.

The personal tragedy and ruin of it all are coming to the fore as the time comes for the great wrench, for H.I.M. to leave. In recent weeks I am told he has been receiving old friends and advisers whom he hasn't seen for decades. People whose advice, whose caution, whose criticism he had rejected – while he went his own way. One such, a close confidant of his father and of himself as a young man, spent an hour alone with him recently after twenty-seven years without meeting him (he had been excluded because too frank in his comments, too troublesome in his criticisms). The Shah was deeply moved and kept falling into an agony of remorse, locking his hands and grinding his knuckles into his palms. Both wept at the end.

So it is this slow, agonising, indecisive, uncomprehending end to the whole Pahlavi adventure. How much, how very much is due to his own personality and temperament: his fatal insecurity leading at once to overcompensation in ambition, ceremony, grandiosity; and at the same time a corrosive mistrust of all around him so that, classically, he surrounded himself with flatterers and listened only to what he wanted to hear. Yet for all the extraordinary and orchestrated campaign of hatred for him, and for all his aloofness and arrogance, he is such a well-known face and presence that his departure is going to be deeply affecting. Many in fact are sorry for him as a person, and inclined to forgive.

Behind him he will leave an instability that we are only beginning to feel now. The well-meaning attempt by Bakhtiar seems so ineffective, so lacking in force. It is the 'tidy' reformist solution. His followers overestimate their ability to ride the popular tiger that Khomeini and the National Front have released. They tell themselves it can be appeased, dispersed and eventually harnessed.

The greatest weakness is the defection and flight of the very middle classes the Shah built up. He allowed them no participation, no responsibility, only the chance to gain prestige and make money. So when the latter was thrown into doubt there was no loyalty, no involvement with him. It was a casual relationship with the regime, not a contract or a commitment. As someone remarked, 'Looking round, who are those Iranians who are still here? It is often the "old families", those who were scorned and derided as "the Thousand Families". It is they who show a patriotism and a hope in Iran's ability to re-find itself, and a determination to see it through. And who are the legions of the opposition? Not the peasants (no), nor really the workers (apart from oil). They are the part-educated – the teachers, the clerks, the engineers, the white-collar and frustrated minor intelligentsia. It is they who are enraged, bitter, vicious – together with the school kids prancing alongside for the fun.'

The grey, chill, dark storm has cleared and the moon is out, gleaming on the snow. Tomorrow will be pristine and brilliant in the cold sunlight – and it will be very difficult to realise these dramas and tragedies are really being played out.

FRIDAY, 12TH

Obvious evidence from the papers that even Khomeini's writ is already failing to run. He commands strikes to continue: they don't. He commands strikes to end: they don't. He orders good Muslims to desist from violence and not attack Savak offices: they don't. Instead one learns more of the guerrilla groups (the Islamic Mujahedin-e Khalq and the Marxist Feda'yian-e Khalaq). The worry is clearly communicating itself to the Khomeini circle. With so much right on their side, they have nevertheless unleashed the tiger. They were warned but what else could they do? Now they see the whirlwind they could yet have to reap.

The crass way the US government has now announced it is in effect dropping the Shah is in the worst tradition of Vietnam and Ngo Dinh Diem.[9] Not only does Vance announce his approval but says the US government 'concurs' with the Shah's decision to leave. Why should it be up to them to concur? Why make it obvious that the Shah is their man? And they then go on to give poor struggling Bakhtiar the kiss of Judas.

With the herd gone, one becomes more conscious of individual decisions to go. Now one hears of enquiries about sending out dogs and cats. Ominously Lufthansa has run out of pet cages!

Most agree Sanjabi is too old, too vague and foolishly over-committed to Khomeini. The name mentioned most should Bakhtiar fail (and the army not then to intervene) is Bazargan,[10] who is said to enjoy genuine religious support. He is also mentioned as a key man for the Regency Council together with Amini.

SATURDAY, 13TH

A fascinating day. The moves towards a climax are under way. Yet in town one drew hope. The crisis has shown that Tehran is either a traffic jam, or else deserted, save for the transitional hour between the two. Today it was back to near-jams, despite the massive serpentine queues at the petrol stations. Everywhere people were glued to their radios to hear Bakhtiar's programme. It proved a feast of things that a month ago would have seemed inconceivable. The people at all levels felt hopeful, reassured. A sense that things could yet come back to a tolerable normality.

There is a resilience here. The sap cannot be kept down but rises at the first relenting of the frost. Central Bank, part of the customs, power workers – all in part started up again. Could Bakhtiar – speaking a clear, forceful, deliberate Persian – yet bring the magic off by producing a constitutional change of regime of revolutionary significance? Yet the shadow remains of the unrelenting power of Khomeini. No serious clergy are in the Regency Council – whose membership gradually came to light in the course of a hectic evening of telephoning. It is a council cobbled together of old hands with a genuflection to each of the main interest groups: the Shah, the army, the *ulema* (only a shadow), the old Mussadeq National Front. Yet a weak thing commanding little respect. Against this is an increasingly windy Majles which sees the Shah is about to go and that it will then be exposed, not only in position and property, but in person. And more disconcerting is that this must apply to the senior army generals too; they are all of a piece with the regime, and they too feel threatened.

To add to the tension and drama, Khomeini announces an Islamic Revolutionary Council (that is, a provisional government) in Paris which would draw up a new republican constitution, ready to move in when Bakhtiar fails ... or even if he succeeds. Finally there is the fairly definite news that the Shah is to leave with all due ceremony and propriety on Monday morning. What a drama this is! Even Shakespeare could not have bettered it.

My heart refuses to surrender to the worst; but my head fears that good intentions are not enough and that the regime and we, 'the collaborators', are going to have to pay for our alleged misdeeds and misjudgements.[11] Much darkness in our chilled house today, alleviated in part by our cheerful log fire. And the first thing to hit one as the power comes back on is not the lights but the Schubert or Bee Gees (as may be) that suddenly starts up from the silenced record player. Faces light up, smiles spread. Life is back; the sun has come out.

SUNDAY, 14TH

A check to one's revived optimism. Judy, my wife, insists that
whatever the apparent facts, Iranians are not reasonable and are
people of extremes. There is no reason to suppose that Khomeini,
and even less the schemers around him – whether they turn out
to be determined Muslim radicals or insidious Marxists using
religion as a cloak (the two hotly contested rival schools of
thought) – will forgo a revolutionary triumph at this point and let
Bakhtiar take the trick and the credit from them, and then meekly
and reasonably work with him for a better Iran. Just to state the
idea shows how grotesque it is on every historical parallel.

In Judy's view the moment the Shah goes, three things will
happen. The social class depending on his regime, mainly our
friends (inevitably) and including the senior generals, will panic
and either run out of fright or lash out desperately to try and
preserve the situation (that is, a coup). And Khomeini will come
triumphantly back to be greeted by hysterical millions, not in lone
splendour but with his train of advisers and associates (that is, *his*
provisional government); at which point Bakhtiar will be shown
to be flotsam on the storm-tossed waters and instantly forgotten
by the people now leaning towards him in the giddy excitement
of the moment. I fear she may well be right. So one's cheerful
humour is snuffed out and one reverts to a leaden feeling of
apprehension.

MONDAY, 15TH

The climax is nearly on us. One thing seems certain: the army is
softening. From all parts of town accounts come of fraternisation
between troops and demonstrators, with carnations being show-
ered on the soldiers or stuck in the muzzles of their guns. Of
tanks with posters of Khomeini pasted on their sides, even of

laughing soldiers handing out portraits and saying that 'K' is their leader. Too late to retrieve this by any hard-line policy now. Meanwhile the senior ranks are demoralised. A leading hawk confessed to me privately that he could no longer be sure of his troops as they were bewildered now that the Shah was going and were being affected by the fervour of the people.

Details and rumours come in of the Shah's planned departure, with proper honours, after the confidence vote in the Majles. It could be tomorrow then, or more probably Wednesday. Only the the Empress, the Queen, remains with him; the rest have gone. Meanwhile the optimists draw strength from the ever-stronger showing of Bakhtiar in the Senate. And clear signs that the strikes are abating in some sectors, though all the stronger in others (all telex out, and power worse than ever, which may however be technical failures due to recent avalanches having brought down power lines in the Zagros).

The fear is of the mass emotion that Khomeini has conjured up – disciplined though it is to a remarkable degree – and still more of the patently clear organisation that lies behind him. Will he be satisfied merely with his return and having a general influence on events? Or is he bent on purging the system, on liquidating a class as in Ethiopia or Cambodia (each, surely, too crude an example), and on launching an Islamic crusade?

If one is inclined to the former view, one has only to talk to people who work within ministries to learn how the management have been astonished at the radicalism among their formerly docile and cowed middle and junior staff; and how these clerks reveal they have been following every deal and transaction and noting how it was corrupt or how reports were falsified! All of this comes out in mass staff meetings in the canteens or in the courtyards. These people are not going to be easily quietened.

First news of Khomeini's Council of the Islamic Revolution:[12] himself, Dr Yazdi, Bani-Sadr, Sadegh Ghotbzadeh (allegedly Leftist),

Admiral Madani and Engineer Bazargan. Yesterday an ominous new wall stencil appeared, sprayed in black: an outline of a guerrilla fighter holding his automatic aloft, with the slogan *Afzal ul-jihad* (The better for holy war). Fear grips again. Has one left things too late?

TUESDAY, 16TH (26 DEI 1357)

At eight minutes past one o'clock midday, the Shah left (*Shah raft*). On hearing it on the telephone from the Inter-Con came that sudden droop I recall having in the old days on hearing that a condemned man had been hanged at dawn in Wormwood Scrubs prison.

To the last it was a mixture of spoof, dignity and force. The press had been told to expect a press conference at the palace at 10 a.m. Only certain journalists were invited, and the unlucky ones fought like furies to get on the bus that was sent. Finally they left ... not up the hill to the palace, but out to the airport. Anticipation grew. Was this it? Yes, it was. At the VIP lounge, cameramen, the Imperial Guard, Court dignitaries were drawn up.

They waited. Nothing happened. At 10.30 a spokesman calmly told them the departure was cancelled – till tomorrow perhaps. Consternation (in truth, I learned today that the Shah had been too overwrought to face the press). Then, shortly before 1 p.m., helicopters clattered and throbbed over my house in the bright sky, now partly clouded. In fact he left (together with the Queen) unobserved by the curious but with full honours – the PM, the Minister of Court, Speakers of both Houses, etcetera all in attendance. By 2 p.m. it was on the news. Even up in chic Elahieh, cars started honking and tooting within minutes. The euphoria was on. Now what of the Old Man in Paris? Can he be humoured to accept the great work Bakhtiar has done in seeing the Shah off?

Or will he release the seven avenging furies of popular revolution?
A new chapter opens.

To herald all this, the latest 'supernatural' event occurred:
yesterday all over Iran the faithful believed they saw Khomeini's
features on the surface of the moon. And yet another earthquake
struck Khorasan. Oh Iran, what a year of events! But to return to
the popular reaction. Irresistible not to go out. Scenes of great
excitement in the streets round us. Every car hooting rhythmically,
flashing its lights. Crowds gathering at every junction: men grin-
ning and giving the V-sign; girls in *chadors* singing and laughing;
boys prancing about shouting at us to put on our lights or to slap
pictures of Khomeini on the windscreen; groups shouting 'Everyone is free now'; small demonstrations brandishing portraits of
Khomeini aloft crying, 'By the force of Khomeini, the Shah has
fled.'

We worked our way up through an old village district by then
in a ferment of excitement and joy. Out onto Pahlavi Avenue where
boys came up hammering on the bonnet advising us to put our
lights out as ahead were 'friends of the Shah': troops. Generally
things became more subdued as we reached Tajrish Square. The
reason was soon obvious: we had to go through a cordon of stern-
looking troops – no flowers here – who were smashing windscreens
with staves if one had one's lights on or a portrait of the Agha on
the car. So past a few truckloads where there was no joy or fervour.
On to Niavaran and a turn round the palace, still bravely flying the
pale blue imperial standard ... but now empty. Unbelievable.

Then back into Khomeini country through the Chizar district.
Lights on again, the honking renewed and we were back in the
seedbed of this revolution – the alleys, bazaars and villages of old
Tehran, alive with kids and teenagers jumping on garden walls,
piling high on the roofs of vans, shouting their heads off, brandishing carnations and gladioli or portraits of the Agha (and
occasionally one of scholarly, bespectacled Shariatmadari) shower-

ing sweets on passing cars. Into the militant village itself which was smothered under slogans on the walls and plastered with that ominous black stencil of the victorious guerrilla brandishing his gun. Past my friend Goudarzi's mosque with about a hundred youths, boys, and girls in headscarves, shouting in unison and brandishing their fists: *Allah-u akbar, Khomeini rahbar* (God is great, Khomeini the Leader). Freedom had come; restraint had finally gone. Well, we'll see. The next few days will show. I myself doubt if Khomeini or his advisers will now relent one jot.

Finally as we reached home I felt as I knew I would feel: that I could take no joy in their joy. Are we faced with a victory, or even the beginning of a victory, of the great conspiracy against the West and of the resurgence of Islam? I have to give way to fears because one has to make personal decisions based on them: I fear Bakhtiar cannot last a week and will be swept aside. This worry was reinforced by a talk tonight to a clear-eyed German who has worked for many years running a farm in the countryside not far outside Isfahan. He has watched the events touch and then seize his own community. He remembers the day when a young mullah arrived in the village from Qom – not a complete stranger but a man who had distant antecedents there. Within days the subversion began: slogans on walls, talks to villagers, sermons by loudspeaker against the Shah and the government which recited all the simple themes we have learnt to know so well (and all of which we have a conscience about): the exploitation of Iran's oil, the corruption, the transfer of ill-gotten gains abroad, army brutality, the corruption and obscenity of Western culture, etcetera, etcetera. Night after night, until 1 a.m., the loudspeaker blared out. And slowly the people turned.

Over weeks the village was politicised and my German friend – from being a popular benefactor and friend – found himself seen as an enemy. Yet he is one who had sympathised with them over the excesses and exactions they had had to undergo from a corrupt and arbitrary authority. He is one who was appalled by the clumsiness and coarseness of the huge American community in the vicinity which swamped the Iranians by its numbers and acted according to the worst canons of insensitive foreigners, even colonialists.

WEDNESDAY, 17TH

The morning after. Fever abated, leaving a city plastered with pictures of the New Leader in abundant poses: the famous posture squatting under the apple tree in his Paris garden, and endless variants of the stern, determined visage. The ruins of the revolution are the stumps of the once-proud statues, their pedestals now scrawled with slogans and covered in portraits, with a queer Islamic pennant or else a black banner stuck on the empty plinth. Youths were still scrambling over them and waving flags on high, but most were excitedly posing in front for memorial scrapbooks as they might in front of Nelson's Column. Everywhere the crowds are kids or young roughneck teenagers, but behind are the bearded student marshals, now suddenly got up in olive-drab army jackets.

The front of the university is seething revolution, with green flags, red flags, black flags, tens of hundreds of pictures of the Old Man, with an occasional hammer and sickle. Nowhere to be seen is any sign or mention of Bakhtiar (or the National Front for that matter) – not even to curse him. He might not exist. All is attributed to the Imam. The papers are full of that heart-rending, melancholy, but punctiliously correct departure of the Shah. Of his last look at the Elborz over his shoulder.[13]

I remember so clearly on that exultant evening yesterday after the Shah's departure, that as we drove up the lanes of Maqsudbeg, the joyous ones were rarely over twenty and often in their early teens, and that on one corner stood an old wizened greybeard who, when I mouthed the question through the closed car window, 'Well, what's all this about?' merely shrugged in a baffled, hopeless kind of way and dolefully shook his head.

Speculation now centres on whether Khomeini is to return, and when. Some enter a new phase of wishful thinking that he won't from fear of being lost among the other ayatollahs. No such fate for such a magnificent and unbending campaigner! Of course he will come but only when he has swatted Bakhtiar aside ... and the army too.

One of the best things of recent weeks has been the controversy at uptown parties. Everyone says they must not discuss politics – and then immediately does so. It is the stuff of life. Before, almost everyone was a grey area in this field – they said nothing on anything that mattered. The only ones whose views one really (presumably) knew were the courtiers and obvious Establishment figures – and even here one sometimes wondered. Now everyone is forced to show his true colours or – more likely – his medley and confusion of colours (at least in the circles we move in).

THURSDAY, 18TH

Carter now calls on Khomeini to 'give Bakhtiar a chance' and crassly asks him to desist from violence (he who has been calling, ostensibly at least, for an end to it). Sounds like pleading from weakness with the man who holds the trumps. But how can Khomeini compromise? It is the conflict between the ghost of a monarchy to which Bakhtiar is committed, and an Islamic republic which the masses are told they want. Only two things can restrain them: fear of the army's reaction; and pressure from the US which even Khomeini recognises he has to work with if he is not to fall under Russian influence. Surely the Saudis and others must be urging him to this? This must make him show his true colours.

In retrospect the mood today in town was like a hangover. One relived the night before, but without the fervour. People seemed dazed, desultory, uncertain. Even at dinner parties, Bakhtiar is simply not mentioned. Not even curiosity about the names or positions of his new ministers. Everyone assumes it is transitory – with hope that this good, brave and honest man is not afterwards branded a quisling.

Such contrary emotions on the Shah's departure. So many confess to weeping on hearing that he had left. Somehow, despite his aloofness, his arrogance, his manifest errors, the evils done in his name and – make no mistake – under his direction, this still youthful, fine-looking man who had been part and parcel of the lives of the great majority of Iranians since childhood, is felt for. People wanted to love him, but he didn't invite it. And now they see he was human and no mere police brute, into which role he is now being cast.[14]

More stories of the 'revolutionary committees' (*komitehs*) forming in each bank, ministry, government agency, even embassies. Junior, disregarded clerks, holding their seniors to account – and being well briefed to do so. So far much of it seems only half-serious, part-imitative comic opera ... until the bloodletting begins.

FRIDAY, 19TH

Gloom setting in, anxiety increasing. More and more, people are coming to realise how trapped their possessions at least are, if not themselves. How all their work is expiring in front of their eyes and they are realising that unhappy decisions are going to have to be taken with increasing rapidity – if it is not too late already.

The first house in our area was ransacked this week (Reza Fallah's)[15] and papers were searched. The Imperial Club was shut and locked yesterday, with something like a hundred private houses marooned in the grounds. No more golf or tennis! Today another mammoth march is to take place, with the avowed aim by Khomeini of ousting Bakhtiar. At least Shapour enabled the Shah to leave constitutionally – in so far as that matters. A great deal, I think, as it prevented an outpouring of venom and violence whose effects would have been irreversible.

More accounts of revolutionary committees in the ministries and agencies. Somewhere about the fourth rung down, they summon their seniors before them to be harangued, castigated, and interrogated on past malefactions and misjudgements. Part play-acting, part deadly serious. When the hard men under Khomeini come in, it will cease to be play-acting. And they are now showing themselves: Dr Yazdi, Bani-Sadr and Ghotbzadeh. Soon we will see the true colours of it all.

Fun among the gloom over the unofficial changes in street names. The street that was called Khiaban-e Taj (Crown Avenue) had scrawled over it Kh. Amameh (Turban Avenue).

An engineer was telling me that the Russians have pulled no one off their sector of the gas trunkline, though they sound as worried as the next capitalist man or company about whether they will be paid, get goods cleared, fuel or raw material supplies delivered, etcetera. And their senior embassy personnel give the impression at least of being as uncertain and apprehensive of the outcome as the rest of us.

Comments and emotions are centred on the overthrow (correction: 'departure') of Muhammad Reza Shah, but the people know that it is the Pahlavi dynasty that has gone. The greatest statue-toppling scenes occurred in fact over the giant equestrian statue of Reza Shah in Sepah Square, and over the standing statue in 24th Esfand Square. I heard that the latter had been defiled and shot at when down and then carted off to Behesht-e Zahra cemetery and given a mock burial. And the Shah's own statue on Avenue Mirdamad was dismembered and its trunk dragged the length of the boulevard.

Yet as some names die, others reappear. Back after twenty-five years is the Il-Khan of the Qashqa'i, Nasser Khan himself,[16] already reclaiming his ancestral home, the Bagh-e Eram, which the Shah had used as his official residence when visiting Shiraz or as a concert hall for the now-notorious Shiraz Festival. What a ferment of excitement there must be among the tribes! What arms will be coming out of cover, or smuggled across the frontiers. The gendarmerie must be fleeing for their lives as the tribes take confidence again.

Many accounts of the great Arba'in march[17] today. Subdued, disciplined, peaceful. Wholly dominated by Khomeini who is being romanticised as a near Godhead. 'God, the Qur'an and Khomeini' instead of 'God, Shah and country', the crowds shout. The Mujahedin-e Khalq much in evidence. Marxist? Or radical Islamic?

The emissary from the Regency Council to Paris is reported to have been spurned. The only thing Khomeini and his friends must be wary of is the army. Some imagine them pulling back in order to strike. Others see the generals as too demoralised, the lower ranks as subverted, and the younger officers and the men as likely to go over to the people. Certainly it is true that many of the lower ranks, conscripts at least, are deserting.

SATURDAY, 20TH

So the great phenomenon inexorably sweeps on. He means every word he says, make no mistake. He fervently, solemnly, magnificently believes in the worth and justice of Islam, and in its benefit for the people, and in its ability to adapt in part to the modern world. But can it ever hold together, or can it only unite to destroy? I suspect it can hold and *might* then be livable with, at least as being stable and not too obscurantist.

The town is flat, grey, shut up, untidy, tawdry with black flags, enlivened only by the endless portraits of Old Beetle Brows. As one observer remarked, if ever there was a case of one Godhead replacing another! Bakhtiar continues to speak out sanely and sensibly – all that Iran needs, but he can do so little without the clout of the millions. The senior men come to the ministries but can do nothing as everything below is seething rejection of all past authority. Administrative anarchy.

Tonight doubts put to rest: the Agha has announced his return 'within the next few days'. It will surely be Saturday, the anniversary of the death of the Prophet and the martyrdom of Imam Hassan. Will the army permit it? Will the same control and discipline be possible? It will be as Lenin's dramatic return by train to Russia in 1917.

SUNDAY, 21ST

Seemingly a quiet day. One new phenomenon is springing up around town: the Islamic co-operatives. Simple, open-fronted bazaar-type shops selling foodstuffs to the faithful at cheap prices. What an organisation this is!

As against this high ideal, it is quite clear that a not-inconsiderable number of those in the perpetual benzene queues later siphon off the petrol they obtain and sell it at black-market rates (× 10 at least) – and then return to the line the next day.

MONDAY, 22ND

Now the secular Marxist groups are showing their strength and scuffles are developing. Girls, unveiled, in blue jeans, hold hands in the processions with their brother comrades (there have always been a high proportion of women activists in the guerrilla shoot-outs reported over recent years). The army sounds confused and divided. Hardly capable of decisive action. And what would they do with it if they had power? They had it before, after all, under Azhari, but the Shah had restrained them then.

TUESDAY, 23RD

The next storm of winter is on us and snow is falling steadily. Yet nothing can chill the anticipation of the Agha's return. Fever is mounting. Historically there can have been nothing like it since Charles de Gaulle strode down the Champs Elysées in 1944.

As Khomeini and his aides make more and more pronouncements, my impression of their sense of purpose, their programme and their essential moderation grows. If they can keep the allegiance of the millions they have aroused (Islam will take care of that) and produce good men to execute their policies, I have no real fears for the country; indeed I think in time it could possibly be a saner and more sensible place. Enlightened Islamic rule as such does not deter me – if it exists. That is the rub, that is the rub.

I still believe the Russians are standing back, and the signs of their reported withdrawals of inhabitants from border villages support the view that they are apprehensive about crusading and resurgent Islam in Persian- and Azeri-speaking areas of Central Asia.

We could be seeing a manifestation of the resurgence of wider Islamic identity and culture, based on new oil wealth and stimulated by excessive exposure to an alien culture, principally Western (but also Russian). Pakistan, Turkey, even Egypt, Saudi itself, and of course Libya and the Palestinians all show signs of it.

It could yet be Europe that gains from all this – France, Germany, even confused old Britain, suspected and trusted, hated and loved, for politics or for myths that are rarely of its own making. God bless the BBC – and the quiet diplomacy behind which Owen has sensibly retreated (unlike the still-sermonising Carter). My only prayer is that retribution is not sought on that brave, true man Bakhtiar. A consummate operation so far, though how he gets out of the apparent confrontation between regency and republic, I don't know – but I guess he will. And I do believe Iran will hold together.

As Khomeini has emerged, however, people are becoming apprehensive of this old religious magistrate who will brook no dissent. One dictator, they say, for another. A facile comparison: the Pontiff of Qom issuing his encyclical and admonitions (they say Shariatmadari will vacate Qom to make room for Khomeini and then return to his own native Azerbaijan)!

The great Iranair jet (formerly the Shah's) is being readied and it is reported that the air traffic controllers will break their strike in order to get the Great Man safely down onto the tarmac. The streets along which he is to pass are being scrubbed. Meanwhile it continues grey and snowy.

WEDNESDAY, 24TH

So it isn't going to be so easy after all. Bridget and our two dogs were due to leave today but a call to the airport at 6.30 a.m. revealed that the army had 'taken over'. Immediately one had the usual multiple explanations: to force Khomeini to do a deal; to prevent a vast and unruly concourse coming to meet him; and to prevent trouble by airport strikers.

Probably, the second is correct but shows how edgy it all is. Did one not take Bakhtiar's words seriously enough? Or General Gharabaghi's – that they will not stand down? And never forget that the Shah, confidence and venom clearly returning, can use the telephone? I draw most hope despite it all from Bazargan's olive branch (or plea?) to Bakhtiar personally yesterday.

The Old Man is already beginning to sound a bit of a handful. Righteous, inflexible, unyielding. He wants to make sure of establishing his dream of a pure Islamic republic (never implemented since the seventh century – as if back to the early Christian fathers) while he still has years left. He wants to leave nothing to chance.

Thus he dare not lose momentum, so insists on coming back so soon against the cautioning of Bazargan and others ('this new extravagance' was Bazargan's despairing comment).

My guess is they will have him back, see him lorded, honoured and revered as never before – and then hope to pack him off to Qom. He may think he can continue from there as in Paris but probably does not realise how heavily dependent he is on his public relations aides and their brilliant propaganda. If by then most of these are ministers and find him interfering tiresomely, they can simply impede the broadcasting of his pronouncements and so let his image fade. He will never have the power and impact he has had in Paris – unless his lieutenants will it so and find him still essential to prosecute the revolution.

THURSDAY, 25TH

Confusion complete. It looks like farce but in fact is deadly serious. The airport closure shenanigans are clearly a power play. Bakhtiar and/or the army are trying vigorously to raise centrist 'constitutional' support at the eleventh hour.

Bakhtiar has written a skilful letter (so respectful one can almost detect the tongue in cheek) to the venerable Ayatollah saying in effect: I will formally resign but will continue to caretake until we can have a referendum on the constitution (that is, the monarchy) and general elections, *provided* you desist from announcing a revolutionary council and delay your return for three weeks. Khomeini and co. say they are flying in regardless – now by Air France charter. Meanwhile the stars came out again last night and today is once more cold, crisp and brilliant.

Talked to a beautiful lady architect last night, highly emancipated. She had returned to Iran three years ago with great hopes but had been quickly disillusioned and then disgusted by the corruption and professional frivolity she had found. She was accordingly sympathetic to the changes under way and thought they would eventually lead to the type of Iran she wished to work for. She was hopeful (as I find many of the best are).

She said she was not alarmed by the prospect of a more restrictive attitude to women under an Islamic order. For one thing, Khomeini's pronouncements on this had been fairly tolerant and reassuring. Frankly she would in any case prefer to dress more discreetly and have less token equality with men if in return she was given proper respect and honour. The so-called freedom of women under the Shah had come down to a debased, up-for-grabs, carefree attitude. Ever since her return she had never been able to sit alone or with a girlfriend without being persistently solicited. She was not worried for the future – and if Khomeini and his men tried to restrict her professional opportunities (which she did not believe would be the case), she would protest and agitate along with many others.

Theatrically, the night of decision. The challenge must come tomorrow if it is to come at all. Either the tens and hundreds of thousands descend on the airport in fury and frustration and overwhelm the troops by fraternisation – in which case it is over for authority and Bakhtiar; or else the troops shoot them down and a hopeless, destructive civil war begins. Or they hold off, and grumble and curse, but do not challenge. In which case Bakhtiar and authority will have won and a decent compromise with Old Beetle Brows will be possible.

Further confirmation comes today of the division in the ministries and agencies at about the fourth level. Vociferous, impassioned but ignorant – with a few senior men opportunistically now jumping on the main bandwaggon.

It is also interesting to speculate on the French role in this. No one comments on them, the protectors of the Agha. Yet enough evidence exists of the hopes of commercial and political advantage from all of this. They are the only bankers and contractors we hear of with hopes. Some say that they became sour with the Shah on the downturn of their commercial expectations; and that the nuclear project is so vital to the French nuclear industry and its future that they will chance a throw on any regime that is likely to keep it going.[18] I do not believe this any more than I do the spurious and mythical 'hidden hand of the English' (which *I* at least know is not there); I think they are just handling a very hot potato that has fallen into their lap with the opportunistic skill and diplomacy for which the French are always given credit.

FRIDAY, 26TH

This was the day Khomeini was to have returned. It ended horribly with the worst indiscriminate shooting from provoked troops. Very ominous. What looked as if it was going through was blocked. Endless speculation as to whether it was the army presenting a *fait accompli* to Bakhtiar (the man they most hate but whom the Shah told them on leaving they had to work with), or a joint action to force Khomeini to do a deal. I suspect the army must have forced the issue to some extent. The sequence of events at the airport seems to have been a refusal to allow Iranair to fly two Boeings to Paris to fetch Khomeini unless the airport staff lifted their general strike; a rallying of people to the airport for a sit-in; movement of troops to block the people coming; and the closure of the airport: block to Khomeini.

Then the accounts of the Constitutionalists' march backing Bakhtiar – a seeming mixture of the old order with a surprising and genuine following of professionals, intelligentsia and middle class who want constitutional rule, many a republic, but none an Islamic republic. All drummed up in two days. Participants hotly deny any government instigation. Some violent sentiments of opposition to Khomeini are expressed, even to the extent of civil war. This was the first attempt by the 'silent majority' (that is, the

Western-educated middle class) to resist the trend, which itself is partly class-based. But worthy though it can be, how can the silent majority pit itself against the millions now aroused?

After today I fear we are in for outright, merciless revolution and a bloodbath if the army resists further tomorrow. The march alone shows the cleavage between the workers, clerks and peasants on the one hand and the flower of the last thirty years of Westernisation on the other. In short, there is a clear class division – the latter a class Khomeini would no doubt like to destroy.

I fear the military (though no doubt flagrantly provoked and taunted by eager martyrs) yesterday have destroyed the burgeoning consensus. The first slogans of 'Death to Bakhtiar' appeared; and Sanjabi, his friend for over thirty years, denounced him as 'a Savaki' – the worst of crimes.[19]

But what else could a good man have done? It was like a Tehran traffic jam where everyone snarls and no one moves. Then one man steps forward and directs it – and, lo, it is free in five minutes. No doubt Shapour saw his role as this; but, to switch the analogy, it is dangerous to bid three no trumps when you only have eight points in your hand and your only court card is a Jack. How he is finding this out near the end of the hand when he has won the (relatively) easy trick.

I cannot believe sensible, astute Bakhtiar favoured such a stupid, no-win tactic. I expect that if you create loyal, brainwashed automatons like the Imperial Guard (the Javidan in particular), you risk some lunatic response.

Many signs that Bakhtiar does not know what he is doing (or what he wants to do) and that he has fallen into the hands of the wild men in the army. One nasty development last night: three Germans playing cards by an uncovered window in dark, silent Farmaniyeh[20] were shot at through the window (one wounded). Is one surprised? This is next to that revolutionary village of Chizar where I first saw those chilling wall stencils of the armed guerrilla (even more of them yesterday, and more slogans than I have seen anywhere else) – and Farmaniyeh is an area of rich villas, now for the most part deserted. Empty streets, stray pets and a few servants, with only the occasional house occupied. Eerie.

Tonight: the airport is closed 'indefinitely'. Incredible: that a modern state can play cat and mouse with thousands of legitimate travellers as part of a checkmate with a political opponent. Surely the diplomatic corps and even the UK must make formal representation to the government? It is no longer just a matter of personal inconvenience. Only the Iranians could be so obsessed with their own problems that everyone else can go hang. One sees it every day in Tehran traffic – someone has an accident and no one else matters even if the jam is a mile long.

On that last Swissair plane out, they say, on Thursday, Bakhtiar's son flew out of the country. To Paris?

SUNDAY, 28TH

The economic consequences of these self-inflicted wounds are beginning to show. Companies are laying off staff wholesale and making drastic cuts in the salaries of others – and this in the midst of crisis inflation rates. Within two or three months, real destitution and hardship are going to hit the cities; if distribution breaks down, there could be starvation in the countryside and towns, now so dependent on imported grain paid for and subsidised out of oil revenues. Yet always in Iran there is this difficulty of taking anything very seriously. There is even the sick joke that the Ayatollah and the Shah will meet secretly in Paris and then return together on the same plane announcing on arrival, 'Dear friends, it was all a joke!'

Today more scuffles in town (a real shoot-out, as it later transpired, at 24 Esfand Square) which madly led to twenty deaths. Cars suddenly begin to honk, flash their lights, and youths come tearing past in cars waving bloodstained shirts and shoes out of the windows. Students now write slogans in their friends' blood and surround the stains on the pavements with flowers. A car was left burning outside the Inter-Continental and no one paid a whit of attention to it. This incredible jape of the airport being closed (though the thought of being trapped in an increasingly dangerous situation is beginning to worry people) while Bakhtiar and Khomeini test each other's wills.

Now the saga of the mountain having been prevented from coming to Mohammad, Mohammad very respectfully suggests coming to the Mountain (in Paris)! Bakhtiar writes and speaks so well and straightforwardly, but the Old Man sounds quite unbending and inflexible.

Tonight the shouting has begun again. The deaths of today. All so perilous, even yet.

MONDAY, 29TH

What I saw the fringes of yesterday turned out to have been the biggest pitched battle yet with troops positioned on rooftops and a concerted attack by the guerrillas on the gendarmerie HQ. It all looks so stupid: kids and boys deliberately bait troops – a dangerous lark – and then, victory achieved once they have a corpse or an injured man for their pains, scream rage at the brutal tyrants and dash around town demanding sympathy and help. It is an effective political tactic though: given the ever-present press to report it, is not as senseless as it looks.

This man Khomeini has truly built himself up, or rather been built up, into a monster, even if a loved one. Even if they wished to discard him for the sake of a compromise, they cannot. He is the high priest of the millions in a vivid, personal, frightening way. He will not be put down. He is magnificently clear-minded, single-minded and unswerving. Having gone so far, don't weaken now, is his constant message. There must be anxiety in his camp that once he is back without a clean sweep of the board, his charisma will quite quickly be eroded through having to live in the real, practical world and having to deal with his fellow aya-tollahs – and so lose his private 'cabinet' who protect him.

On, off: Bakhtiar to Paris tomorrow; Khomeini to Iran. Despite the posturing and play-acting, could there still be a sensible deal between them? I believe their common interests and attitudes are far greater than their divergences. I suspect that they are each being tugged back by their hotheads: Khomeini by the discordant advice of Yazdi, Ghotbzadeh and co. who clearly – and typically – are fall-ing out among themselves; and Bakhtiar by the hawks of the army who may well be in touch with an embittered H.I.M. I heard one theory that, now sitting in Morocco, he was fed exaggerated reports of the Constitutionalists' march as being a pro-Shah march – which it was in sections only. And he may have encouraged the senior generals to crack down and try to 'restore' the situation – when all they have done is seriously to exacerbate it ... but I doubt it.

Nor should one underestimate the effect of such heady triumph on a vengeful, ambitious old man. Not likely to induce a spirit of compromise.

A big fire in the south west of town. Huge columns of smoke which I later learned was our dear old Shekoufeh No music hall and the red-light district behind it being 'cleansed' by fire because the Agha's route would pass near it on his way to Behesht-e Zahra cemetery.

WEDNESDAY, 31ST

A depressing call on a former (indeed still) high official. He and his wife alone and forlorn in their fine house, now devoid of ornaments, pictures and rugs – the instant tell-tale signs these days of imminent departure.

The same talk: uncertainty, anxiety, reluctance to leave as it meant abandoning most of their possessions. My friend, however, now bore the mark of Cain: he had been on the List. At first he had laughed it off as preposterous, but soon he came to see it was not a matter of simple truth or falsehood. He had been irretrievably smeared, and he was then to pay for it. He was hauled up before an upstart committee of radical half-bearded youths from his own ministry and from Central Bank and interrogated, insulted and told the burden of disproof was on him.

The house in question was on 'Nob Hill' in Elahiyeh and soon whole areas of similar districts are going to be deserted, left to become the haunt of stray dogs. What will the revolution do with the houses? Or will there just be a change of owners? Tonight the rumours of the imminent return of Khomeini ('the Agha', to use Goudarzi's kindly and respectful title) began again. So the last week of delay, killing, mounting ferocity and stupidity was as futile as it always seemed. The army has said it can no longer hold the streets (or hold its own men) and the government is clearly resigned to his return.

FINALE

We leave. Off to the bear-garden of the airport at 7 a.m. on a crystal-clear morning with fresh snow on the mountains like icing on a wedding cake. The millions have not yet begun to congregate for the Advent tomorrow morning, but there was nevertheless a thrusting, pushing, aggressive jungle of chaos at the airport. No panicking, yet everyone very determined. Japanese, Germans, Koreans, British, Americans – the legions of the failed White Revolution – all running. Yet who outnumbered them ten to one? The files of Iranians waiting in humiliating line for their passports, stacked in racks.

It is ironical that although the whole movement was unleashed (but not created) by Carter's human rights crusade – to which the Shah felt it politic to show some token response – the Americans as a whole have taken the stick for it. Simple slogans are the stuff of the masses so there is no differentiation between Nixon, for example, an arch exponent of the old order, and Carter, who well-meaningly but unwittingly unleashed the tiger. Another ironic feature is that the habitually chaotic, undisciplined, violent Iranians are remembered most of all from recent events for their mammoth, disciplined and peaceful marches. Any lessons? Without the Mosque, disorder; with the Mosque discipline and organisation and order? We'll see.

So finally out we flew over the great arid vastness of the Iranian landscape laced by dry riverbeds, relieved from time to time by some tiny isolated, cubist village far below, itself no doubt aflame with Khomeini's pictures and slogans. And dramatising it all, the harsh white ridges of the winter mountains and, in the West, the deserts of the high unbroken snowfields of Kurdestan.

Tomorrow he, the Agha, flies in over this, seeing once again this dramatic land; and carrying with him a burning fixed intention to exact vengeance, expunge fifty years of falsehood and create a new, pure, just order of a restored and, he affirms, enlightened Islam.

If ever one volume closed and another opened, it is on this, the last day of January 1979.

EPILOGUE

An Islamic Revolution and Its Aftermath

Thus, we left Tehran on 31 January. Yet it was impossible to put the drama we had left behind out of our minds. I tried to maintain the diary, but it was pointless when I was no longer an eyewitness.

On 1 February Khomeini made his fateful flight to Tehran by Air France.[1] The ayatollah's last words on leaving French soil were to thank his hosts 'for their understanding of liberty'. His first public pronouncement in Iran was uncompromising as he threw down a challenge to the Bakhtiar government: 'Resign or be arrested.' The perverse symmetry of these two utterances was not lost on us.

The events culminating in the undisputed transfer of power to the new revolutionary regime in mid-February are well known, as are the subsequent episodes in the life of that regime – the hostage crisis, internal power struggles, purges and assassinations, the eclipse of the secular politicians, the murderous Iran–Iraq war, the branding of Iran as a pariah state bent on furthering its interests through means fair and foul, and subsequent attempts by the US to 'contain' Iran. But reviewing my perceptions of a generation ago, as reflected in this diary of those last five months of the Pahlavi era, it is worth looking back on some of the judgements, hopes and fears I expressed at the time.

One thing emerges clearly: when I saw the Priest as invincible,

I was right – and this from the earliest days, as much a gut feeling
as a rational one. And when I saw the King as vulnerable, again I
was right – and from the very outset. But when I allowed myself
to believe, to hope, that the good men of the centre would
somehow get their act together, or that the halfway house of
Bakhtiar might succeed at the eleventh hour, I was wrong.

My anxieties, however, about a descent into general mayhem
were belied. To a remarkable degree the whole saga seemed under
broad control, with the heat turned up or down as required.
Things never got really out of hand until the final two days – and
then it was all over. But I was right that the key to it all was the
attitude of the Iranian armed forces – and that these had looked
unreliable for months.

I never shared the views of some that Ayatollah Khomeini was
too ancient, too out of touch, and that, from some sanctuary in
holy Qom, he would be content to preside over, but not rule, what
he had unleashed (US ambassador Sullivan for one had cherished
the hope that he might prove to be some Gandhi-like figure!)
From his first words one was struck by his single-mindedness, his
implacability, his fierce puritanism and his commanding authority.
Here was no ducking-and-weaving politician but verily a man of
religion with a will of iron that never wavered. This impressive
combination – the like of which had not been seen in the West for
centuries – is what struck the world, such was the force of his
personality and the impact of his brooding image.

As for the poor Shah, it was patently downhill all the way, with
scarcely any phases when he appeared to regain his grip, much
less wield an iron hand – it was just not in his nature: he displayed
simply bafflement at the scale and force of what was happening
beneath him, with a consequent loss of confidence and decisive-
ness. Fitful half-measures, all too late, were the order of the day,
forced on him by events. In retrospect it is a wonder that the
weakness and indecisiveness of the man had not been spotted

before by all – including the United States and British governments – who took his braggadocio and posturing at face value.

And what of all the talk, so dear to most Iranians, of foreign plots? Was the hidden hand of the British behind all this? Decidedly not, not even an empty glove. Still, the charge that the BBC fuelled events from afar, though implausible, caused enough anxiety in London to lead to an internal inquiry at the BBC. It concluded that though the World Service's Iranian exile commentators may at times have allowed themselves to be carried away by events back home, there had been no conscious attempt to breach the BBC's policy of objective reporting. And no one could even imagine there was some devilish US plot behind it all. Patently the State Department, National Security Agency and Pentagon were at sixes and sevens.

And the Russians, or Soviets as they then were? My words show I always doubted the Soviet hand in this for they risked destroying a devil they knew (and not such a bad one either from their point of view) and gaining a far more dangerous one in a militant Islam which they have since had to live with in a disturbed Central Asia. So schooled was one in the Cold War days, however, to see a Soviet hand behind almost everything that at times I too succumbed to suspicions and anxieties. But as has become clear, they were almost as baffled as we were seeing their Leftist lackeys cast aside and then eliminated.

What then of the arch-schemers of all in many Iranian minds: the international oil companies? There never was any gain for them in the destabilisation of the Shah's regime for they had no idea of and no control over whom they might have to deal with in succession. Aghast, they too watched from the sidelines the wreck of a working (if at times, fractious and expensive) relationship – and then had to live with years of disruption to their markets and the immense physical destruction of their assets in the Iran–Iraq War (another consequence of these events not lightly to be overlooked).

In brief, conspirators, if and when they conspire, must feel certain of the outcome of their conspiracy. We must assume that the various candidates of the conspiracy theorists in the pantheon of plotters – be they British, American, Soviet or dastardly oil companies – must at the very least have recognised this truism. But the outcome of any plotting in Iran was never likely to be certain. And the turbulent and far-reaching after-effects of the revolution have more than amply demonstrated how unpredictable the disruption of Pahlavi Iran was likely to be. No outside forces would have dared to risk their existing assets in Iran – be they political and commercial as in the case of the West, or stability and predictability on their borders as in the case of the Soviets – on such a gamble.

The events of 1978–79 led not just to a convulsion in Iran – to the destruction of a whole social, professional class and its diaspora in hundreds of thousands to the USA, to Britain, France, Germany, Turkey and most corners of the globe (perhaps some 1–2 million people left, largely from the middle classes) – but also to what may prove to be the most lasting effect of all: the rise of an emboldened, determined, militant Islam on the world stage, prepared to renew battle with its age-old enemy of the Christian West and its modern secular turpitude. The fervour of the militants may be checked, may run out of steam; but it may not. It is still too early to say but without doubt the ferment whipped up in such countries as Algeria, the Sudan, Pakistan, Afghanistan and, most menacingly of all, in the Lebanon and Palestine through Hezbollah and Hamas, would not have happened at all – or certainly not with the speed and in the form it has – without the dramatic triumph of a radical, fundamentalist Islam with its swordbearer, the Ayatollah Khomeini, bringing down in the space of a year the seemingly invincible and well-armed regime of the Shah of Iran.

Yet for all that, the wave of revolution that Khomeini and his followers called for did not happen: the Persian Gulf, Iraq, Egypt,

Saudi Arabia were rocked but held. In fact almost the entire Muslim world is still ruled by the same regimes that ruled a generation ago. The Muslim dominoes did not fall. No Islamic crusade against the West and its puppets swept all before it.

I end this retrospect – and this book – on a note of hope with the concluding passage of a talk I gave to the Royal Society for Asian Affairs in February 1980 not long after my return. I said then: 'Nothing is ever clear-cut in Iran, not even between enemies. So it has been in all history. Continuity has been Iran's lifeline, no matter what compromise, hypocrisy or double-think has been necessary to achieve it. I therefore do not doubt that a less rigid, less bitter Iran will eventually re-emerge, but not for a long time and until it has painfully worked off its complexes in strutting but illusory self-assertion and its need for vengeance.' While this outcome between the Priest and the King was crystal-clear, the result of that outcome is still not clear-cut.

Notes

September 1978

1. The flamboyant Shahyad arch was created by the Shah at the apogee of his powers on a vast roundabout on the road from Mehrabad airport into central Tehran. Loosely translated, the name means 'A Memorial to Monarchy'. Extravagant and grandiose in style and seen as the very epitome of the regime, it surprisingly came to be adopted by the revolutionaries, not least because it initially offered a splendid surface on which to scrawl slogans and graffiti! It still stands – now called Borj-e Azadi (Freedom Arch) – having clearly won a permanent place in Iranian hearts, and is as much part of the Tehran scene as the dome of St Paul's is of London

2. Jaleh (strictly Zhaleh) Square is in the older part of downtown Tehran in the east near the parliament buildings. It is now called Martyrs' Square (Maidan-e Shohada).

   The number of dead was first officially put at 58, then revised to 95, then to 110. The rumours began at 250, rose to 1,000, and eventually reached 3,000. The action began at 9.20 a.m. under General Ovaissi as Martial Law Commander.

3. The journal began as no more than this – simple diary jottings.

4. The Shah's brothers, sisters and dependants, who tended to be spoken of as separate from himself, had been the open butt of criticism for many years. Not only were they wont to flaunt their wealth and power, but they had carved out lucrative niches for themselves in property, construction and industry, and were often the key to the awarding of contracts.

5. With the huge growth in the number of business expatriates working in Iran (some 60,000), an army of servants had come to work for them when demand outstripped Iranian supply: Filipinos, Bangladeshis, Afghans, etcetera. We employed two Bangladeshis in the end, who feature later in the story.

6. The Persian Service is one of the longest-established vernacular

services broadcast in the BBC World Service from Bush House in London. It was perceived by most Iranians to play an exceedingly important role in the revolution. Iranians had always been prone to spot a dastardly British hand in key events in their country. Now was no exception and no amount of explanation of the independence of the BBC from the British government could eradicate the view that through the BBC the British were attempting to influence events. Having said that, it had to be admitted that on several occasions the Persian Service's reporting did seem rather to relish the Shah's difficulties (see also the entry for 25 September).

7. The Shah's long-standing, close but secret relations with Israel were often the target of political criticism. There was an unacknowledged but open Israeli 'delegation' in Tehran which in effect operated as an embassy.

8. These rumours were the first indications that an organising hand was at work on the revolutionary side. There were also rumours that Yasser Arafat had his men there.

9. Moharram is the yearly period of religious mourning for the death of Hussein, the Prophet's grandson, in 661 AD. Demonstrative processions and passion plays at this time of year are a traditional part of the Iranian scene; the Shah had allowed their revival in recent years after decades of repression as some form of safety valve for the religious elements, showing that he did recognise the religious as a force that had to be conciliated or at the very least kept quiet, and also as a bulwark against communism.

10. The Shiraz Festival was an ambitious attempt promoted by the Empress and the Court Minister, Assadollah Alam, to put 'modernist' Iran on the international cultural map. Far removed from Tehran and far removed in price from the man in the street, they were seen by critics as the visible evidence of the foreign-loving elite (*farangi-ma'ab*) who went to see 'degrading' displays of advanced Western theatre, dance and music which were shocking to the traditional puritan Muslim ethos ... and sometimes even to Western eyes.

11. A reference to Princess Ashraf, the Shah's twin sister, and a strong personality and political figure in her own right.

12. On 20 August the Rex cinema in Abadan had been burnt down; the blaze incinerated some 450 trapped inside. It is now known that the fire was started by a man acting alone but within the general climate of the revolutionaries' call to destroy cinemas and other symbols of the hated West. However the mullahs were quick to exploit the situation by pinning the blame on Savak – and hence the Shah. They succeeded: he

never recovered from this charge in the eyes of the masses. A most successful if brutal ruse.

13. The Majles is the lower house of the Iranian parliament (in the Shah's time there was also a Senate as an upper house).

14. Pahlavi was the name adopted for the new dynasty by Reza Shah in December 1925. It is also the modern name for the principal language of ancient Iran. When Reza Shah was attempting to create legitimacy for himself in the 1920s after usurping the Qajar throne and crowning himself as Shah, the deliberate choice of such a pre-Islamic name for his new dynasty, echoing a previously glorious era of Iranian history, was part of his public relations grand design.

15. Haldeman and Ehrlichman were Nixon's right-hand men who were ultimately dropped during the Watergate affair as he attempted to stave off defeat by dropping his advisers.

16. Mohsen Pezeshkpour, the leader of the ultra-nationalist Pan-Iranist party in the Majles, and one or two other deputies such as Ahmad Bani-Ahmad, appeared to be bravely pushing against the boundaries of free parliamentary debate. With hindsight they were no more than a vehicle by which the regime permitted some steam-letting. It was all to no avail as the revolutionary groups had little time for them.

17. Sharif-Emami, who had been prime minister in the early 1960s and had family connections with the clergy, was brought back as prime minister by the Shah on 27 August following the Rex cinema fire when he dropped the liberalising Jamshid Amuzegar. Sharif-Emami had also been head of the Pahlavi Foundation which made him irrevocably a Shah's man in the people's eyes.

18. The Shah had been prevailed on by pressure from President Kennedy to appoint Amini as a reformist prime minister in the early 1960s (he held office May 1961–July 1962). The Shah had never trusted Amini, whom he regarded as 'America's man'. Amini had been out of power and away from the mainstream of Iranian politics for a generation – the entire period during which Iran had emerged as a main player in the region and the Shah had presented himself, with help from syco-phants, as a world-class statesman. Amini's readiness to dismiss the Shah's more extravagant notions did not appeal to the King of Kings.

19. This was the period of Soviet-backed coups in Kabul and Addis Ababa.

20. This was a rare and – as it proved – revealing address to the people at large.

21. The Shah's arbitrary decision to abolish the ages-old Islamic solar calendar was widely unpopular (and scandalous to the clergy). The Shah was ordering the abolition of the only calendar everyone had ever known, and its replacement with the Shahanshahi (imperial) calendar based on the putative date of the foundation of the great *pre*-Islamic – the important point – and purely Iranian Achaeminid dynasty some 2,500 years earlier. People were both offended and baffled to wake up one morning and find themselves living in 2535 not 1355! This not only enraged the mullahs but led many ordinary Iranians to question the sanity of the leadership, let alone its wisdom and good judgement.

22. His Imperial Majesty, the formal abbreviation by which the Shah was often referred to in English (in Persian, it was *A'lahazrat-e homayouni*).

23. These were two contemporary parallels. And so it proved to be.

24. Mansour Rowhani was latterly Minister of Agriculture.

25. Amir-Abbas Hoveyda was prime minister from January 1965 to August 1977 when he was appointed to the almost equally powerful position of Court Minister. He was dropped on 10 September as part of the signal the Shah was attempting to give in the direction of reform.

Hoveyda himself was an honest and capable but a very pliant bureaucrat who was well versed in the infighting that went with retaining the Shah's favour. Many hold his spinelessness in the face of the Shah largely responsible for Iran's fate. This is only a little exaggerated.

26. This became the appeal on the streets to the Shah's troops: 'Soldiers, you are our brothers.' Over time it worked.

27. A devastating earthquake occurred on 16 September in the remote central desert town of Tabas. Emergency relief organised by the mosques proved far more effective than the much-heralded efforts by the government, not necessarily because of a lack of government effort, but because the clergy were quicker to spot the public relations advantages of this disaster.

28. This was the first mention in my journal of the priest himself, Ayatollah Ruhollah Khomeini, and of Ayatollah Kazem Shariatmadari, not his rival as such but the leading spokesman in Iran of a more conservative but still highly critical group of clerics.

29. This was the explanation circulating at the time. It has since become known (Daniel Drooze's article 'The CIA's secret IRAN fund', *Politics Today*, Santa Barbara, Ca., March–April 1980) that covert US payments had been funnelled to the clergy through the Court since the Shah's restoration in 1953 as a means at once of keeping the mullahs

sweet and of strengthening them as a naturally anti-communist element in society.

It was only with the advent of Jimmy Carter that all such hidden subsidies were abruptly halted, but as this more or less coincided with the advent of the 'pro-American' and more strait-laced Amuzegar, it was widely assumed that the decision was his. It is asserted that this sudden withdrawal of subsidies and favours did more than anything else to lose the Shah the support of the more moderate and passive body of leading clerics (mullahs) and push them towards the intransigent Khomeini.

30. The young Nasir ud-din Shah had his chief minister put to death in January 1852 in the Bagh-e-Fin garden in Kashan whence he had been sent after falling from the Shah's favour

31. Like so many cities, Greater Tehran was formed from a number of formerly outlying villages which were absorbed as the city spread, yet kept something of their old identity.

32. The Shah's eldest son, Crown Prince Reza, was eighteen at that time. Following the Shah's death in exile in Egypt in 1980, this well-meaning but ineffectual young man proclaimed himself Shah.

33. A novelty for Tehran – and a conspicuous part of the process of Westernisation – was the establishment of a full-blown racecourse and public stands in 1976 by a Hong Kong group. By 1978 the racecourse was becoming popular across the classes. In a diminished form it has survived the revolution because camel and horse racing is not frowned upon in the Qor'an even though gambling is!

34. The Kourosh store was one of a new chain of foreign-style super-stores and was seen as a prominent example of Western materialism, as were banks, cinemas, liquor stores and the like, which hence were prime targets of the riots.

35. Now the Esteghlal (Independence), the Hilton was the first and most prominent of the new US-style hotels. It was built in the 1960s far out of the centre of town on the hills close to Shemiran.

October 1978

1. The Shah and Queen Soraya fled to Rome, spending only three days there before returning on the back of the successful uprising against Mussadeq on 15 August (28 Mordad) 1953, which the CIA, with crucial help from their British friends, engineered.

2. General Ne'matullah Nassiri had been a rather oafish but ruthless head of Savak (the national security and intelligence organisation) for the previous eight years. Before that he had been successively Chief of the Imperial Guard and Chief of Police. Replaced as early as 6 June 1978 as an early concession to the unrest, he was packed off as ambassador to Pakistan. He returned voluntarily if imprudently on 7 October to face investigation as the pressure on the Shah mounted, and he was arrested on 7 November. He was among the first to be executed on the night of 15 February 1979 after the collapse of the regime.

3. The second holy city of the Shi'as in Southern Iraq (the other being Karbala), a little-known backwater where Khomeini lived and preached in exile from 1964 to 1978. He was nevertheless a sharp thorn in the Shah's side from there. It was only when, of his own volition, he moved to Paris that he became accessible and a magnet attracting world-wide media attention and political support.

This had been brought about by a visit to Najaf from Paris of all three plotters (Dr Ibrahim Yazdi, Abol-Hassan Bani-Sadr and Sadeq Ghot-bzadeh) who had seen his potential as a revolutionary figurehead. Kuwait first refused him entry. The party retreated to Basra, from where a visa to enter France was sought from the French government (who first checked directly with the Shah that it was in order to issue one). This granted, the party then flew from Baghdad.

4. General Fereydoun Djam was an upright and highly respected officer of the old school who, as Chief of the Imperial General Staff, had fallen out with the Shah and been dismissed, although later given a diplomatic post as ambassador to Spain. On returning, he went to live in Paris and now London.

5. Ardeshir Zahedi was a former Foreign Minister and high-profile, party-loving ambassador to London and then Washington. A key figure as a young man with his father, General Fazlullah Zahedi, in the August 1953 (28 Mordad) coup against Mussadeq. He was reputed to have been the principal vehicle through whom the CIA mobilised the downtown demonstrations clamouring for the Shah's return.

6. One of the two English-language daily newspapers in Tehran, published by the Ettela'at group, the other being *Kayhan International*.

7. As a protest against growing censorship and restrictions, the entire press went on strike on 11 October. The government in effect capitulated on the 13th.

8. The Shi'a mourning tradition is to commemorate a death forty days after a funeral. The strike was called by Khomeini from Paris.

9. Liz Thurgood, at the time and still in retrospect, was the best-informed foreign journalist on the opposition and one of the most perceptive commentators.

10. Houshang Nahavandi, an oily and ambitious Establishment man *par excellence*, had been chief of the Empress's Bureau and latterly Minister of Higher Education, and had emerged as the 'safe' spokesman of the liberal tendency in the ruling group.

11. Jebhe-ye Melli was the main grouping of liberal, nationalist and religious parties that had its origins in Mussadeq's time. Since 1953 it had been persecuted and hounded and its leaders were periodically imprisoned. It now had the opportunity to make a well-based organisation of itself but suffered from persistent internal dissension as it was a coalition of parties, not a party in itself.

12. In a widely publicised statement, Dr David Owen, the British Foreign Secretary in James Callaghan's government, had dubbed the revolutionary religious movement as 'right-wing, reactionary and fanatical'. This really got under the opposition's skin.

13. The lower house of the Iranian parliament.

14. The original red rag to the revolutionary bull was an unsigned article published in *Ettela'at* on 7 January slurring and slighting Khomeini, particularly with remarks about his mother. It is now known the letter was inspired by and emanated from the Court and had the Shah's personal hand in it. The government, and in particular the Minister of Information, Darioush Homayoun, knew nothing of it until it appeared – though the authorship was widely attributed to him.

15. The then French President, Valéry Giscard d'Estaing, was suspected by many of playing a canny hand of reinsurance against the possibility of the Shah's overthrow and declining health, for all his oft-professed support of him in his glory days. The fact is that within two weeks of Khomeini's arrival in Paris on a simple foreign visitor's visa and not as a political refugee (on which he would have been subject to specific constraints), he had twice been rapped over the knuckles by officials and cautioned against advocating organised violence in Iran, yet on the 19th could be found giving an interview to *Le Figaro* and broadcasting on state television denying the Left or the communists were with him, questioning the loyalty of the Iranian army and threatening the ultimate sanction of an armed uprising!

However, the memoirs of the Comte de Marenches, who paid a secret visit to the Shah, together with Poniatowski of the French Foreign Ministry, throw an altogether different light on this matter. They show that on the one hand the Shah would not sanction the French authorities dealing with Khomeini more forcefully on the grounds that he was less trouble in Paris than he might be elsewhere, and on the other that he was not prepared to sanction harsher action against his own people. He was directly in touch with Giscard on these matters. The French concluded from this recipe for inaction that his days were therefore numbered and Giscard reported as much to the summit meeting of Western leaders in Guadeloupe the following month.

16. The population of Iran was then some 30–35 million. Since the revolution it has had one of the highest growth rates in the world – 4.2 per cent – and has reached over 60 million in only eighteen years.

17. The modest head covering, well short of a full veil, called *ru sari* (on the head), was increasingly adopted by young girls and women during the growing unrest of 1978 as a symbol of opposition. It is now widely in use. Like the full *chador*, it is part of *hejab*, the discreet Islamic covering of women.

November 1978

1. In recent years a radical new thesis has been advanced that there was no irreconcilable conflict between traditional Islam and secular Marxism (this was the theory that the Shah sneered at and disparaged as 'Islamic Marxism'); and indeed that one could modernise within Islam without 'Westernising'. The great advocate of this thesis was one Dr Ali Shari'ati, a young intellectual who had caught the imagination of the devout Muslim youth who were yearning for a new creed that was not communist but that did not deny the advantages of modern living. In the 1970s he preached and taught in particular at the Husseiniyeh Ershad mosque on the Old Shemiran Road which became a hotbed of barely tolerated dissent and excitement.

Shari'ati died in Southampton in June 1977. (Many believe – entirely wrongly – that he was eliminated to order. In fact he died of a heart attack.) The bands of guerrillas who were thorns in the security forces' side in the late seventies usually called themselves Islamic Marxists.

2. Dr Muhammad Mussadeq was the former nationalist prime min-

ister under whom the Shah was forced to leave the country in 1953, only to return three days later at the head of a US- and British-inspired assisted coup (28 Mordad) which resulted in Mussadeq's overthrow and imprisonment. Mussadeq spent the rest of his days under house arrest on his own estate.

3. Amini's first meeting with the Shah in 1978 was on 3 November.

4. Dr Ali-Naghi Alikhani had been a youthful Minister of Economics in Hoveyda's government and later President of Tehran University; he had always been thought of as something of an Establishment liberal. Charismatic, intelligent and capable, Alikhani was viewed with suspicion by Hoveyda, whose scheming had led to his withdrawal from public life. Since the revolution he has edited and published the diaries of Assadollah Alam, his mentor.

5. One of the three principal Western-style hotels established in the late 1960s and 1970s, the others being the Arya Sheraton (now the Homa) and the Hilton (Esteghlal). The latter was in the hills near Shemiran in the north, the Inter-Continental downtown, and the Sheraton was in Vanak. The pack of journalists covering the gathering revolution made their base principally in the 'Inter-Con' – as it was commonly referred to – downtown.

6. Karim Sanjabi was one of the most senior and long-lasting of the National Front leaders from Mussadeq's time. Often imprisoned, he paid a fawning call on Khomeini in Paris and encouraged the strike movement on his return on 10 November. After the revolution he was briefly Foreign Minister before being humiliated by Khomeini and thrust back into obscurity and irrelevance. He went into voluntary exile.

7. The Bashgah-e Shahanshahi was founded in 1971 on the hills above Vanak as a country club of a kind Tehran had not seen before. Smart, opulent and exclusive, it was a common meeting ground for Iranians and foreigners, a place where the rich, the newly rich and the aspiring rich came to see and be seen.

8. A principal east–west road of the time on the outskirts of the central area.

9. Bank Melli was the principal state-owned commercial bank; NIGC was the National Iranian Gas Company.

10. The Chieftain tank was then the latest British army battle tank. The Shah demanded that the engine, turret and gunsight be modified to meet Iranian conditions as he saw them.

11. General Ali Khademi was the founding father of Iranair and a much-respected figure as a professional man.

12. The young British-educated water engineer who became the technocrat Minister of Water and Power.

13. Houshang Ansari, the former Minister of Finance and latterly chairman of NIOC, was widely thought of as one of the smartest and most powerful of ministers – and the one who had made the greatest fortune of all.

14. Ashura is the tenth day of Moharram (the 'Good Friday' of the Shi'a calendar), the day in AD 630 that the Third Imam and grandson of the Prophet, Hussein, and his family were done to death on the battlefield (at Karbela in present-day Iraq), having been denied food and water in the searing heat of the desert by the armies of the Caliph, whom Hussein and his followers regarded as a usurper. Thus were born the symbolism and traditions of the Shi'a – all very appropriate as symbols of the battle against oppression that Khomeini was now leading.

15. The two principal skiing areas are now Dizin and Shimshak. The first had been at Ab-e Ali to the east.

16. This was an enterprising and lively young Second Secretary, David Reddaway, who was one of the Persian-speakers in the embassy. After the revolution, he later returned as chargé d'affaires in Tehran from October 1990 to June 1993.

17. After our first diplomatic posting in Iran (1958–62) and before our second (1971–74), my wife and I had spent four years in Kenya in the British High Commission immediately after independence in December 1963.

18. Gholam-Ali Ovaissi was army commander and Abbas Gharabaghi was his Chief of Staff. Ovaissi had been Military Governor of Tehran during the Jaleh Square massacre; the revolutionaries labelled him 'the Butcher of Jaleh'. A tough talker, he revelled in his reputation, especially after the revolution when he attempted to bring together anti-Khomeini elements in Paris. He was assassinated there in November 1984.

Gharabaghi, a more diplomatic and mild-mannered officer, later became Chief of Staff and can be credited with reducing bloodshed in the critical days of early February 1979 when he withdrew the army from confrontation with Khomeini's people in the streets.

19. General Fazlollah Zahedi was the strong-man general behind the successful army coup in 1953 which overthrew Mussadeq and restored

the Shah. Street gangs financed by his son Ardashir with CIA dollars were paid to clamour for the Shah's return with cries of 'Javid Shah' (Long live the Shah).

20. This was Khodadad Farmanfarmaian, a former head of the Plan and Budget Organisation, and later a governor of the Central Bank and finally chairman of a new private-sector bank, Bank Sanaye Iran.

21. Fereydoun Mahdavi, the hard-driving and progressive Minister of Commerce, was new and younger blood in the cabinet. A strong supporter of the National Front, this capable technocrat had been brought into the government as part of a seemingly enlightened policy in the 1960s and early 1970s to co-opt moderate dissidents into the Establishment.

22. Hassan-Ali Mehran was a young and novel appointment as governor of the Central Bank.

23. This was the veteran, popular and independent-minded oil man Bagher Mostofi, who had been chairman of the National Petrochemical Company since its establishment as an entity separate from NIOC. He was one of the band of young men who had been sent to Europe – in Mostofi's case to Imperial College in Britain – in the 1930s when Reza Shah began the training of a cadre of professionals.

24. Rasht is a large town near the Caspian coast in Gilan. It is the butt of a legion of stories, most of which centre round the ease with which Rashti husbands are cuckolded. A Rashti joke is the Persian equivalent of an Irish joke in Britain or a Polish joke in America.

25. General Mehdi Rahimi was among the first four to be executed after the revolutionaries took power. He was an honest, straight-talking soldier driven only by fierce unshakeable loyalty to the Shah.

26. Younger lawyers in the leadership were Hedayatollah Matine-Daftary and Hussein Lahiji. Mehdi Bazargan and Darioush Forouhar were National Front stalwarts. Bazargan became the first prime minister of the post-revolutionary government and Forouhar became Minister of Labour. Matine-Daftary and Lahiji had distinguished themselves as younger men in agitating bravely for civil rights. All these individuals were rapidly sidelined as the clergy consolidated their post-revolutionary power base, and they are now scattered among the capitals of the West.

27. Adnan Menderes, the long-serving prime minister of Turkey, was overthrown in a military coup, summarily tried, and swiftly executed in 1960.

28. Shapour Bakhtiar was a long-standing and independent-minded National Front politician who had had experience in the French *maquis* during World War Two. He was the son of a Bakhtiari, a tribal leader too, with all that implied in tribal following.

29. Abdullah Entezam, the 81-year-old former Foreign Minister, was highly respected among the Establishment as honest and untainted by Iran's more recent *folies de grandeur*. But an 81-year-old saviour?

30. The Baha'i faith is a nineteenth-century offshoot of Shi'ite Islam. Baha'is are reviled by the Shi'ite clergy as heretics. Often men of ability and integrity, Baha'is had nevertheless achieved a number of prominent positions and were said to have been favoured by the Shah. Hoveyda's father had been one, though the son always maintained that he himself was not. Another was the Shah's personal physician at the time, Dr Abdul Karim Ayadi.

31. The first mention in the diary of the new Chief of the General Staff, a stolid career soldier, Gholam-Reza Azhari.

32. Eid-e Ghadir is the anniversary of the day, the Shi'ites believe, the Prophet appointed Ali as his rightful heir and thus the first Imam. A public holiday in Iran.

33. A joint Irano-British Chamber of Commerce had been established in 1977 and I was its first chairman. Before this there had been only an informal British Businessman's Group whereas the American and Germans in particular, and the French too, had had full-blown chambers.

Kheradjou was the tough, dour, humourless but effective president of the Industrial and Mining Development Bank of Iran (IMDBI) who was respected for his honesty and integrity. But as a proven survivor he naturally had to know the workings of power in the Shah's Iran.

34. Bunyad-e Pahlavi, a foundation of immense wealth to which the crown lands (*amlak-e Pahlavi*) had been endowed. It was involved in a multitude of major ventures in properties and business. Its revolutionary successor in many ways is the Bunyad-e Mostazaffin (Foundation for the Oppressed) owning much the same assets.

35. General Azhari was appointed prime minister of the military government on 6 November, the day after the countrywide riots.

36. The high point of the Moharram mourning period which would begin on 2 December and last ten days.

37. Roloff Beny, a brilliant, showy and very camp photographer, produced a book of stunning photographs of Iran, *Persia: Bridge of Turquoise*,

in which the Shah and all his works were lavishly and sycophantically praised. Beny followed this up with an even more adulatory volume (but again with great photos) called *Iran: Elements of Destiny*.

38. The prime institution, the National Iranian Oil Company, was situated in a vast concrete slab on Takht-e Jamshid Avenue.

39. Dr Manouchehr Eghbal, the loyalist above all, who had been prime minister from 1957 to 1960 and had been recalled to become chairman of NIOC. He died in 1977.

40. Iranian credulity at the influence of the BBC – and of the hand of the British government they unshakeably hold to be behind it – perhaps goes back as far as the BBC broadcasts that preceded the fall of Reza Shah in 1941. Sattareh Farman Farmaian vividly describes her childhood memory of this in her book *Daughter of Persia*: 'Then one evening, a voice speaking in Persian was heard on the BBC from London ... there was a voracious worm (the Shah) in Iran, this accusing voice said ... Clustered around the radio we listened, at first in disbelief and then in growing astonishment and exhilaration. "It's obvious," said one excitedly. "The British have decided to get rid of Reza Shah." ... Now the BBC was shouting openly to the whole country the truths we ourselves had not even dared to whisper.' *Plus ça change*, said the Iranians in 1978!

41. Hojabr Yazdani was an immensely rich Baha'i who had become a financial power in the land, having risen from very humble beginnings.

42. Parviz Sabeti was a senior but comparatively young Savak officer who was widely believed to be in charge of the sharp end of the organisation responsible for internal subversion, imprisonment and, as part and parcel of it, presumably torture. Sabeti was universally feared – justifiably or not – and thought to be the real brains of Savak. He was Deputy Head at the time he left.

43. Club-e Faranse, situated on Avenue Fisherabad. Iranians had long been members and it was something of a social and intellectual centre. The British equivalent was the Tehran Club situated in a more elegant Qajar mansion just off Ferdowsi Avenue but lacking the same social spice and cuisine.

44. My daughter Bridget, then 21, had been living with us for the past two years and working as a secretary. She in fact stayed on and we left Iran together on the last day of January 1979.

45. This was Sir Anthony Parsons, the British ambassador who recorded his mission to Iran memorably in his book *The Pride and the Fall*.

He left Iran on 8 January 1979 only a week before the Shah. He died in August 1996.

December 1978

1. This was the Oil Consortium, established in 1954 as the successor to British Petroleum. It consisted of the major Western oil companies which would periodically negotiate with Iran as a group on oil pricing, payment terms, allocations etcetera. The conspiracy theory was that since the contract with the Consortium was up for renegotiation, it was in the Consortium's interest to see Iran destabilised, especially since Iran was making noises about becoming involved in downstream marketing and distribution – the Consortium's patch.

2. The Tudeh was the offical Moscow-backed communist party of Iran (*tudeh* means 'the masses'). In its legal heyday in the late 1940s and early 1950s, it was the largest and best organised communist party outside Europe. It was crushed and proscribed after the attempt on the Shah's life in 1949 and its principal leaders fled abroad where they were given refuge first in Moscow and then in Leipzig in the German Democratic Republic. From there, with direct but unacknowledged Soviet backing, they ran for many years the most effective of the subversive broadcasting stations, Sada-ye Melli-ye Iran (National Voice of Iran) attacking the Shah and all his works, especially his friendship with the West.

3. The National Iranian Gas Company was the sister body to NIOC. Its founding managing director was Dr Taghi Mussadeqi.

4. Abdul was one of the two Bangladeshi domestics (the other rejoicing in the name of Shashanka) whom we had brought from Dacca when it became impossible to find Iranian staff.

5. General Amir-Hussein Rabii was chief of the air force.

6. General Manouchehr Khosrowdad was a dashing young officer, very close to the Shah, who had created the Iranian Special Forces. To the clergy this proven action-man was the most feared of the Shah's generals, and he was among the first four officers to be summarily executed on the night of 15 February.

7. Kish Island near the mouth of the Persian Gulf had been selected by the Minister of Court, Assadollah Alam, as a site to be developed as a winter resort encompassing all pleasures for the rich of the Persian Gulf and Europe. Mme Claude in Paris, provider of female delicacies to the

world's rich and famous, used to fly out her girls by Concorde to be part of the fun. It was also a lucrative duty-free zone, separate from the mainland. Mahmoud 'Stanley' Monsef was its first chief executive. He was alleged to have absconded with £5 million on 10 November but successfully defended himself in a series of libel actions.

8. The large Muslim population of what was then Soviet Central Asia, divided among the various republics, all of which are now independent states.

9. My office was on the top of a seven-storey block in Khiaban Kheradmand-e Shomali; I could walk out through French windows to see what was going on immediately below, round about and right across town.

10. Some 90 km south of Tehran, the holy city of Qom is the shrine of the Imam Reza's sister, Hazrat Ma'sumeh, and the centre of the leading seminaries and religious colleges of Shi'a Islam.

11. This was John (Hajji) Cooper, now a lecturer in Persian at Cambridge University, who in fact had been not a mullah but a *talabe*, a student who on occasions interpreted for Shariatmadari in his dealings with the international press.

12. A very influential traditional and revered ayatollah at that time resident in Najaf in Iraq where Khomeini had been. He was of the more pacific non-political school.

13. King Hussein of Jordan was a close personal friend of the Shah and was a not infrequent visitor on private occasions. As the principal friends of the West in the Arab world, he and the Shah had many interests in common. King Hussein's last reported visit was as late as 26 November.

14. A former long-serving private secretary to Hoveyda as prime minister, Parviz Radji was appointed ambassador in London after Hoveyda became Minister of Court. After the revolution his revealing memoirs were published as *In the Service of the Peacock Throne*.

15. A holy shrine about 10 km to the south of Tehran, this is where Reza Shah's mausoleum was.

16. William (Bill) Sullivan was the US ambassador over the critical period. He arrived in 1977 and left in February 1979. His own book, *Mission to Iran – the Last US Ambassador*, revealed the extent to which US policy making had been in disarray.

17. Tassu'a the day before Ashura, the ninth day of Moharram.

18. I have regrettably been advised by my publishers and their lawyers to omit this name.

19. The Camp David talks were the critical talks between Anwar Sadat and Menachem Begin, brokered by President Carter, on which world attention was primarily focused at this time. It is arguable that had the Americans not been so distracted by the prize of the Egypt–Israeli dialogue they would not have lost their Iranian jewel. With their eye off the Iranian ball this meant there was no coherent Iran policy, which resulted in internal disagreements and disharmony.

20. Army barracks in the northern part of the city used by the Gard-e Shahanshahi – the Imperial Guard.

21. Qomi was a leading ayatollah of the time. All ayatollahs took their formal names from their town of origin, in this case Qom. The Imam Reza was the eighth Imam descending from Ali, who for Shi'ites was the successor to the Prophet himself. Imam Reza is revered among them in his own right.

22. Admiral Habibollahi was commander of the navy.

23. The northernmost suburb of Tehran at the very foot of the Elborz mountains, Shemiran originally consisted of a number of mountain villages strung along the mountainside at points where streams issued forth. Darrakeh was one such.

24. Parviz Tanavoli was a leading contemporary sculptor.

25. Amir Aslan Afshar was a long-serving and very loyal aide to the Shah. He had been ambassador to Bonn and was recalled late in the day to become Grand Master of Ceremonies under Hoveyda's successor as Minister of Court, Ali-Qoli Ardalan. He left with the Shah and stayed with him in Egypt to the very end.

26. Dr Gholam-Hussain Sadighi: another elderly respected figure with the requisite connections with the National Front (he had been a Minister in Mussadeq's government) who was to have been wheeled in as a liberal.

27. At the time the principal thoroughfare to the north of Shah Reza Avenue which had attracted many of the new modern offices, hotels and shops. The US embassy was situated on the north side. It is now renamed Khiaban Ayatollah Taleghani.

28. A much-loved pastor, Father Williams had baptised my son, Richard, who was born two months after our first arrival in Iran in August 1958, and had later confirmed my daughter, Geraldine.

29. This was the late Señor Aurelio Valls, the Spanish ambassador. Aurelio was a distinguished poet in Spain as well as a diplomat, and he

and his charming wife Carmen used to give some of the loveliest parties, he and she singing and playing the guitar.

30. Khomeini's father had reportedly been killed during Khomeini's childhood in a dispute with Reza Shah's representative in their home town. Khomeini's son, Mostafa, died while they were in exile in Najaf. Khomeini's followers have always maintained that Mostafa was poisoned by Savak. There is no evidence that either died other than a natural death, but the mud has stuck.

31. My wife and I had established a tradition of open house on Boxing Day – people came as they pleased and helped themselves from 12 noon until twelve midnight, in shifts as fancy took them for lunch or tea or dinner or dancing.

32. 500,000 barrels per day compared with a peak of 6 million barrels per day in the boom time.

33. This was the name by which the Shah's father was known as a colonel in the Cossack Brigade before making his coup on 21 February 1921. It was four years after this before Reza Khan became Shah, so ending – in the person of Ahmad Shah – the Qajar dynasty.

34. This is the first mention in the journal of Shahpour Bakhtiar in his new role. His administration was to last thirty-seven days. After escaping from Iran during the revolution he set up one of the principal opposition movements abroad, the National Resistance Movement of Iran, in Paris. He was assassinated in his apartment there by agents of the regime in August 1991.

January 1979

1. Taleghani was one of the dominant early figures of the revolution. He was less dogmatic than Khomeini, and the two later fell out. Taleghani died, some say mysteriously, in 1980.

2. This was Sir Horace Phillips and his wife Idina. Sir Horace, a former senior diplomat in the British Embassy in Tehran (and later ambassador to Turkey), had returned in his retirement to Iran to represent Taylor Woodrow. The episode is described in his published memoirs, *Envoy Extraordinary*.

3. Another reference to my experience of Independence in Kenya in 1964.

4. Rustam Pirasteh was an Iranian who had moved to the US some

years before and had risen fast through the banking profession. He returned to Iran in 1977 to head up an aggressive new joint venture bank with Chase Manhattan. To many people's surprise, he made the bold move to abandon this base and throw in his lot with the 'liberal' group of technocrats around Bakhtiar. I knew him quite well through my banking activities.

5. This was a dream team that was never realised. Bazargan was always with Khomeini; Djam would not commit himself. It is interesting to find Darakhshesh's name as he was a radical Minister of Education in Dr Amini's cabinet of 1961–62.

6. Ahmad Mirfendereski had been Deputy Foreign Minister (and ambassador in Moscow before) at the time of the Yom Kippur war in 1973. As acting Foreign Minister, he had personally authorised overflights of Soviet aircraft to the Arab states without first clearing this with the Shah. He paid for it with his job.

7. Prominent among the pack were R.W. (Johnny) Apple Jr, Eric Pace and Nicholas Gage of the *New York Times*; Jonathan Randal of the *Washington Post* who had sniffed the wind earlier than any the year before; J. Alex Morris and Bill Tuohy of the *Los Angeles Times*, the former to be shot dead in only a few weeks' time during the storming of the air force barracks on 13 February (the only journalist to be killed in the revolution). On the British side was Martin Woolacott of the *Guardian*, Charlie Douglas-Home, Tony Allaway, David Watts and Anthony McDermott of *The Times*, Andrew Whitley and Simon Henderson of the *Financial Times*, David Shears of the *Telegraph*, and many, many others.

8. Mashad is a holy city in the east of Iran, the site of the venerated Imam Reza's shrine. Qazvin is a famous old town some eighty miles to the west of Tehran.

9. Ngo Dinh Diem was the President of South Vietnam, whose overthrow and assassination in a US-inspired coup in 1963 was the precursor of the Vietnam War.

10. Mehdi Bazargan, a veteran figure of the National Front and after 1961 of his own Liberation Movement of Iran, had always been associated with the clerical Right. At that time in his late seventies, he became the first prime minister of the Islamic Republic. He died in January 1995 in Switzerland. The Shah had agreed to the formation of a nine-member Regency Council on 3 January.

11. The ambassador advised all British expatriates to leave at a meeting called in the British Embassy summer compound in Qolhak on 13 January.

12. This was the first mention in the journal of Dr Ibrahim Yazdi who had been living in the US for many years and had been a focus of opposition activities there. He managed to combine a devotion to Islam with the pragmatism of *realpolitik*. Abol-Hassan Bani-Sadr was a sort of economist with a strong religious bent, living in Paris. Sadegh Ghotbzadeh was an opposition adventurer who embraced Leftists, intellectuals and obscurantist priests as it suited him.

Yazdi was to become Foreign Minister, Bani-Sadr the first President, and Ghotbzadeh in turn Foreign Minister. Whereas Yazdi, even when he fell from grace with Khomeini, has remained in Iran, Bani-Sadr fled into exile in France. Ghotbzadeh fell foul of Khomeini on the unpardonable grounds that he was plotting against him, and was swiftly tried and executed in 1982. The three of them were the trio that had persuaded Khomeini to come to Paris after he was denied entry to Kuwait from Iraq. They then orchestrated his propaganda and operational campaign from the French capital and were the most consistently visible face of the revolution apart from the Ayatollah.

Admiral Ahmad Madani was a competent, tough-talking officer who had been dismissed by the Shah for being too critical. He was to become the commander of the navy, the Minister of Defence, and the governor of oil-rich Khuzistan province; but his loyalties to the revolutionary regime were suspect and he too was to end up in exile.

13. The Elborz mountains are the chain (rising to 3,975 metres in Towchal) that runs east–west immediately to the north of Tehran. They make a spectacular backdrop to the city.

14. After a wretched odyssey taking him to Egypt, then Morocco, the Bahamas, Mexico, fatefully to hospital in New York in October (which led to the seizure of the US hostages in Tehran), and then on to Panama, the Shah ended his days in Egypt once again, dying on 27 July 1980. His tomb is in the al-Rifa'i mosque in Cairo.

15. Reza Fallah was probably the most powerful and capable of the oil company's directors. His house was prominently situated on one of the hills overlooking north Tehran.

16. Nasser Khan Qashqa'i was chief of his tribe, a large and nomadic one which in the previous generation had proved a troublesome thorn in Pahlavi flesh.

17. Arba'in is the fortieth day after Ashura.

18. This nuclear project was the French state nuclear company Framatome. On 25 January 1979 the project was cancelled. So much for the

myth. I later learned that the Shah had *asked* the French to take Khomeini – presumably believing he would be silenced there.

19. Savaki was the name given to anyone who was a presumed collaborator of Savak.

20. Farmaniyeh was then a quiet, rather distinguished district of north Tehran.

Epilogue: 1–11 February 1979

1. My wife, daughter and I left on Swissair, touching down at Damascus and then going on to Geneva. The next day we continued to London where we, our two dogs and ourselves landed in a heap, exhausted but relieved. Yet I couldn't tear my mind away from the drama one had left behind and for the next few days I was glued to the television and newspapers watching and following the final acts. Briefly they went like this:

Flight AF4271, an Air France Boeing 747, took off from Charles de Gaulle airport at 1 a.m. on Thursday 1 February. The Ayatollah was travelling in first class. There were a total of 168 on board, most of them journalists. Fuel was taken for the flight there … and then back, just in case.

At 9 a.m. local Tehran time the *Agha*, clad in his now famous black turban and cloak, emerged at the top of the aircraft steps to an ecstatic welcome and Mehrabad airport. After formal greetings and subsequent pandemonium in the arrivals hall, he was installed in a sky-blue Mercedes van and disappeared into a wildly excited throng in the streets of the city to emerge half an hour later by helicopter (because of the crush) at Behesht-e Zahra cemetery to make his first public pronouncement.

For three days deadlock ensued: Bakhtiar continued to make resolute pronouncements, while Khomeini denounced him as 'illegal' and threatened a *jihad*. The first break in the stalemate came on 5 February when Khomeini announced the formation of a Provisional Government under Mehdi Bazargan as its Prime Minister. Bakhtiar dismissed this as a joke but the stalemate gave credence and shape to the mass support clearly evident for the Ayatollah. The erosion of Bakhtiar's position became ever more obvious, even though he boldly held a press conference asserting that he would never yield and promising elections in six months' time … but few were listening.

Throughout all this the attitude of the Army high command remained uncertain. The Chief of Staff, General Gharabaghi, did not come out or act openly in support of the 'legitimate' government – and without clear support from the military, Bakhtiar was patently lost. Meanwhile the rank and file, already of suspect loyalty, began publicly to go over, given a lead by technicians and cadets of the Air Force.

A revolutionary Provisional Government came into being on the 9th and Bazargan made a last appeal to his old political colleague and personal friend, Bakhtiar, to give way peacefully.

Matters came dramatically to a head on the 10th. An Imperial Guard unit sent to quell unrest at the Farahabad air base among Air Force personnel, who had been aroused by watching a film of Khomeini's return, provoked violence. In the fierce clashes that ensued more than a hundred were killed. Word spread rapidly to town, crowds came onto the streets, spontaneous fighting erupted in many places.

At 10.20 a.m. on the following day, 11 February, Gharabaghi suddenly and unexpectedly announced the decision of a council of senior generals that the Army was to be politically neutral and that therefore all military units were to return to barracks immediately. At a stroke the streets were left to the revolutionaries and the people. Bakhtiar quit office forthwith and vanished underground. In effect the regime had thrown in the towel. The mob ruled the streets and armed gangs stormed the now passive Army barracks and bases, seizing arms and ammunition. It was all over.

On the following day, the 12th, it was indeed clear that this was so. The Shah's palace at Niavaran was taken without resistance. Armed groups held sway, seizing and arresting the leaders of the overthrown power. General Nassiri, already beaten and bloodied, together with Generals Rabii, Naji and Khosrowdad were summarily executed on the night of 15 February on the roof of the Alavi School where Khomeini had set up his headquarters the week before. This hard act (with grisly and chilling photographs) more than anything proclaimed what had happened. The Revolution had triumphed and the Ayatollah's longproclaimed Islamic Republic was at hand. It was twelve months almost exactly since those first shots were fired in Qom.

Further Reading

Alam, Asadollah, *The Shah and I: The Confidential Diary of Iran's Royal Court 1969–1977*, ed. Ali-Naghi Alikhani, I.B.Tauris, London, 1991.

Amirsadeghi, Hossein and R. W Ferrier (eds), *Twentieth Century Iran*, Heinemann, London, 1977.

Arjomand, Said Amir, *The Turban for the Crown – The Islamic Revolution in Iran*, Oxford University Press, New York and London, 1988.

Bakhash, Shaul, *The Reign of the Ayatollahs: Iran and the Islamic Revolution*, I.B.Tauris, London, 1985.

Bill, James A., *The Eagle and the Lion: The Tragedy of American–Iranian Relations*, Yale University Press, Newhaven and London, 1988.

Farman Farmaian, Sattareh, *Daughter of Persia*, Bantam Press, London, 1992.

Graham, Robert, *Iran: The Illusion of Power*, Croom Helm, London, 1978.

Halliday, Fred, *Iran: Dictatorship and Development*, Penguin, London, 1987.

Hoveyda, Fereydoun, *The Fall of the Shah*, Weidenfeld & Nicolson, London, 1980.

Huyser, General Robert, *Mission to Tehran*, André Deutsch, London, 1986.

Jerome, Carole, *The Man in the Mirror – A True Inside Story of the Revolution – Love and Treachery in Iran*, Unwin Hyman, London, 1987.

Pahlavi, Princess Ashraf, *Faces in a Mirror: Memoirs from Exile*, Prentice-Hall, Englewood Cliffs, New Jersey, 1980.

Pahlavi, Muhammad Reza, Shah of Iran, *Answer to History*, Stein and Day, New York, 1980.

Parsons, Anthony, *The Pride and the Fall: Iran 1974-1979*, Jonathan Cape, London, 1984.

Radji, Parviz C., *In the Service of the Peacock Throne: The Diaries of the Shah's Last Ambassador to London*, Hamish Hamilton, London, 1983.

Shawcross, William, *The Shah's Last Ride*, Chatto & Windus, London, 1988.

Sick, Gary, *All Fall Down*, I.B.Tauris, London, 1985.

Sullivan, William H., *Mission to Iran: The Last US Ambassador*, W.W. Norton, New York and London, 1981.

Taheri, Amir, *The Unknown Life of the Shah*, Hutchinson, London, 1991.

Zonis, Marvin, *Majestic Failure: The Fall of the Shah*, University of Chicago Press, Chicago and London, 1991.

Index

Afshar, Amir Aslan, 127
Alam, Assadollah, 56, 184
Alikhani, Ali-Naghi, 56, 191
Amini, Dr Ali, 22, 43, 56, 62, 90, 94, 132
Amuzegar, Jamshid, 14, 29
Ansari, Houshang, 63, 81
Arafat, Yasser, 182
Ashraf, Princess, 56, 90, 184
Ashura, 67, 85, 117, 123, 192
Azhari, General Gholam-Reza, 82, 85, 87–8, 94, 127

Baha'i, 81, 194
Bakhtiar, Dr Shapour, 55, 70, 81, 133–4, 138–9, 141–2, 145, 161, 165, 167, 169–70, 178
Bani-Sadr, Abol-Hassan, 97, 155, 188, 201
Bazargan, Eng Mehdi, 78, 81, 117, 152, 156
BBC, 48, 55, 87, 90, 94, 107, 180, 195
BBC Persian Service, 19, 33, 41, 45, 107, 109, 184
Behesht-e Zahra cemetery, 162, 173
Borujerdi, Ayatollah, 29, 79
Britannia, HMY, 98
British Embassy, 19, 59, 69
Brzezinski, Zbigniew, 136
Byrd, Senator Robert, 100

Calendar, Imperial, 14, 24, 186

Carter, President Jimmy, 2, 10, 42, 97, 105, 133, 160, 165, 175, 187
Central Bank, 92, 99, 152
Crown Prince, 31, 51

Dizin, 8, 127
Djam, General Fereydoun, 38, 44, 81, 146

Empress (Queen Shahbanou), 20, 51, 86, 109, 125–6, 155
Entezam, Dr Abdullah, 81, 138
Ettela'at, 12

Farahabad, racecourse, 95
Farmanfarmaian, Dr Khodadad, 193
Farman Farmaian, Sattareh, 195
Feda'yian-e Khalq, 151
French Club, 92
French government, 97, 108

Gharabaghi, General Abbas, 72, 86, 192
Ghotbzadeh, Sadegh, 188, 199, 201
Giscard d'Estaing, President Valéry, 48, 189–90
Goudarzi, Ali, 25, 27, 66–7, 102, 112, 115–16, 129, 143–4
Grimm, Peter, 126

Harney, Judy, 16, 82, 154
Hilton Hotel, 32

Homayoun, Darioush, 189
Hoveyda, Amir-Abbas, 27, 29–30, 103, 115, 186
Hua Guo-feng, 49
Hussein, King, 109
Hussein, President Saddam, 35
Huyser, General Robert, 136

Imperial Club, 59, 161, 191
Imperial Guard, 117, 156, 198
Inter-Continental Hotel, 58, 145, 172
Islamic Marxists, 13
Israelis, 17, 19

Jaleh, 11, 15, 17, 25, 30, 42

Kayhan International, 189
Khademi, General Ali, 62, 64, 81
Kheradjou, Abol-Qasem, 84
Kho'i, Ayatollah, 109
Khomeini, Ayatollah Ruhollah, 5, 12, 14, 29, 37, 40, 45, 50, 54–5, 79, 86, 98–9, 108, 115–16, 123, 129, 132, 141, 143–4, 147, 163, 166–7, 172, 178–9, 181, 199
Khosrowdad, General Manouchehr, 103, 196
Kish Island, 104, 197

List, Central Bank, 90–3, 108, 174

Majles, 20–1, 46, 88, 141
Marenches, Comte de, 190
Marja'-e Taghlid, 79,
Mehran, Hassan -Ali, 76
Military University, 23
Mirfendereski, Ahmad, 144
Morgan Grenfell, 8
Moharram, 33, 77, 89, 98, 184
Mujahedin-e Khalq, 151, 163

Mussadeq, Dr Muhammad, 55, 57, 191

Nahavandi, Houshang, 44
Najaf, 12, 14, 37, 141
Nassiri, General Ne'matullah, 37, 115, 147, 188
National Front, 5, 45, 58, 69, 83, 121, 123–4, 133, 159
Neauphle-le-Chateau, 137
Niavaran, 111
NIGC, 60, 101
NIOC, 89
NPC, 77

oil companies, 41, 90, 99, 126, 180, 196
Ovaissi, General Gholam-Ali, 15, 59, 72, 77, 80, 107, 119
Owen, Dr David, 45, 48, 55, 61, 70, 165

Pahlavi, 30, 185
Pahlavi Foundation, 84
Paris, 37
Parsons, Sir Anthony, 94
Pezeshkpour, Mohsen, 21
Pirasteh, Rustam, 143–4
press, foreign, 93, 145, 200

Qolhak, 19, 67, 101, 128
Qom, 12–3, 108, 158
Qomi, Ayatollah, 118–19
Qur'an, 65, 163

Rabii, General Amir-Hussein, 119, 139
Radji, Parviz, 109
Rahimi, General Mehdi, 78
Rasht, Rashti, 77, 79, 85, 193
Rex cinema, Abadan, 14, 20, 49
Reza Shah, 111, 132
Rowhani, Mansour, 27

Russia/Russians, 42, 51, 85, 104–5, 114, 165, 180

Sabeti, Parviz, 91
Sadighi, Ghulam-Hussain, 127, 131–2, 138, 149
Sanjabi, Karim, 58, 70–1, 78, 111, 137, 152, 191
Savak, 65, 117, 195, 202
Shah, Muhammad Reza Pahlavi, 4, 13, 18–19, 21–4, 26, 31, 36–40, 43, 47, 51, 55, 57, 60, 65, 67, 72, 80, 86–7, 98–9, 105, 113, 119, 122, 126, 128, 149, 150, 161, 179–80, 201
Shariatmadari, Ayatollah Kazem, 12, 29, 32, 50, 71, 109, 166
Shari'ati, Dr Ali, 166, 190
Sharif-Emami, Ja'afar, 14, 22, 32, 43, 81
Shemiran, 121
Shi'a, Shi'ite, 124, 129
Shiraz Festival, 20
Soviet Union, 28
Sullivan, William, 114, 117, 179

Tabas earthquake, 16, 28, 31
Tabriz, 11, 28
Tajrish, 133
Taleghani, Ayatollah, 138
Tanavoli, Parviz, 125–6
Tehran Journal, 41
Tehran University, 13, 49
Thurgood, Liz, 43
Tudeh Party, 4, 45, 102, 104, 124–5, 196

US companies, 120
US Embassy, 60, 180

Vahidi, Dr Iraj, 62
Vance, Cyrus, 136, 152

Whitley, Andrew, 45
Williams, Father, 128

Yazdi, Dr Ibrahim, 155, 173, 188, 201

Zahedi, Ardashir, 38, 42, 44, 107, 117, 133